Heywood-Wakefield Blond
Depression to '50s

Donna S. Baker, Editor

Schiffer Publishing Ltd

4880 Lower Valley Road, Atglen, PA 19310 USA

Acknowledgments

This book would not have been possible without the assistance of the Levi Heywood Memorial Library, 55 West Lynde St., Gardner, Massachusetts 01440. We extend deepest thanks to Director Gail Landy and Local History Cataloger Pam Meitzler for providing access to their wonderful collection of Heywood-Wakefield catalogs and other historical materials. We are also grateful to Travis Smith, Good Eye Mid Century Modern (www.goodeyeonline.com), for providing the furniture values included in this book.

Objects depicted in this book may be covered by various trademarks, copyrights, and logotypes. Their use herein is for identification purposes only. All rights are reserved by their respective owners. "Heywood-Wakefield" is a registered trademark of The Heywood-Wakefield Company owned by the South Beach Furniture Company, Inc. This book is not sponsored, endorsed, or otherwise affiliated with The Heywood-Wakefield Company, South Beach Furniture Company, or any other companies whose products are represented herein. This book is derived from independent research.

Copyright © 2005 by Levi Heywood Memorial Library Association
Library of Congress Control Number: 2005931117

Designed by Mark David Bowyer
Type set in Zapf Humanist Demi BT / Korinna BT

ISBN: 0-7643-2279-6
Printed in China
1 2 3 4

Published by Schiffer Publishing Ltd.
4880 Lower Valley Road
Atglen, PA 19310
Phone: (610) 593-1777; Fax: (610) 593-2002
E-mail: Info@schifferbooks.com

For the largest selection of fine reference books on this and related subjects, please visit our web site at
www.schifferbooks.com
We are always looking for people to write books on new and related subjects. If you have an idea for a book please contact us at the above address.

This book may be purchased from the publisher.
Include $3.95 for shipping.
Please try your bookstore first.
You may write for a free catalog.

In Europe, Schiffer books are distributed by
Bushwood Books
6 Marksbury Ave.
Kew Gardens
Surrey TW9 4JF England
Phone: 44 (0) 20 8392-8585; Fax: 44 (0) 20 8392-9876
E-mail: info@bushwoodbooks.co.uk
Free postage in the U.K., Europe; air mail at cost.

Contents

Foreword

The popularity of Heywood-Wakefield Modern at the turn of the millennium is a great tribute to the talents of the Heywood-Wakefield Company. Although no longer in operation, the company's legacy continues. We at the library of Heywood-Wakefield's hometown are fortunate to have refurbished Modern furnishings (a dining set, lounge chairs, and sofa) in the staff room of our brand new building. This is actually their third library location; they were originally in the Adult Reading Room of our "West Branch" and secondly in the staff room at our previous location. The library staff is pleased that thanks to this text, you will learn much about the Heywood-Wakefield Company and its modern furnishings.

—Pamela Meitzler
Local History Cataloger
Levi Heywood Memorial Library
Gardner, Massachusetts

Preface

"In this little folder, we present the latest designs of Heywood-Wakefield Modern furniture. They are the result of *long experience, top styling talent,* and *good furniture construction knowledge.* It's *sensible* furniture, *soundly built,* planned to meet the needs of our present-day American living…and to do so *attractively, helpfully,* and *economically*… And it's livable furniture that brings to *every* room the charm and comfort which we Americans have always desired throughout our homes."

—Heywood-Wakefield brochure, 1950

There is no doubt that the Heywood-Wakefield Company, a very prolific furniture manufacturer originally based in Gardner, Massachusetts, is best known for its line of sleekly designed "modern" furniture produced from the 1930s through the early 1960s. The vast majority of this furniture was made of solid birch and manufactured using one of two light colored finishes (Wheat or Champagne), hence its current classification as "blond" Heywood-Wakefield. Highly successful in its day, this timeless, well-constructed furniture has enjoyed a renewed popularity among furniture collectors and enthusiasts of today.

Historical Overview

The origins of Heywood-Wakefield date to 1826, when the five Heywood Brothers—Walter, William, Benjamin, Levi, and Seth—began making chairs, a product for which they would become well known throughout the furniture industry. A formal partnership was established in 1835 under the name of B.F. Heywood & Co., and the company would go through several periods of restructuring and name changes over the next few decades.

The Wakefield side of the company's name can be traced to Cyrus Wakefield, a Boston grocery store owner who began selling rattan in 1844, later founding his own company, the Wakefield Rattan Company, Inc., in 1873. Since the Heywood company had begun manufacturing chairs made of reed and rattan in addition to wood, the two contemporaneous firms enjoyed a good-natured but competitive rivalry that ultimately led to their consolidation as one company, Heywood Brothers and Wakefield Company, in 1897. Following the acquisition of two other entities—the Oregon Chair Company in 1920 and Lloyd Manufacturing Company in 1921—the entire firm was reincorporated as Heywood-Wakefield Co., a name that remained in place until the company's final closing.

Heywood-Wakefield's manufacturing line continued to focus primarily on chairs and related products, such as seating for schools, theaters, trains, and buses, until the early 1930s. (The company was also well known for its production of baby carriages and doll carriages.) As the trend in the 1930s shifted toward the manufacture of complete suites of furniture for the home, however, Heywood-Wakefield followed suit, becoming one of the first furniture manufacturers of the era to offer—as described in a 1951 address by then President Richard N. Greenwood—a "complete and harmoniously designed furniture 'package'."

Initially, the company's foray into complete furniture lines focused on the Early American style, a style already in use for many of the chairs being produced by Heywood-

Wakefield. "Then, with the wider acceptance of contemporary design, loosely called Modern Furniture," notes Greenwood in the same 1951 address, "we embarked on the manufacture of what was then called Streamline Modern and Swedish Modern furniture. In fact, we became in 1931, the first manufacturer to produce furniture of contemporary design on a production line basis."

That first line of contemporary furniture was produced in collaboration with well-known designer Gilbert Rhode, the first of several important designers of the era to work closely with Heywood-Wakefield. Other designers credited throughout company literature with creating various pieces or entire lines include Russel Wright, Leo Jiranek, Alfons Bach, Count Alexis de Sakhnoffsky, Ernest Herrmann, and Joseph Carr. While each designer naturally retained an individual style, Heywood-Wakefield prided itself on the fact that all pieces—regardless of design origin—could be incorporated successfully and pleasingly into any room of the house.

"Four different designers created the five pieces shown in the above living room corner," states Heywood-Wakefield in its 1939 catalog. "Yet note how perfectly balanced this group is from a design standpoint and how Heywood-Wakefield furniture blends and harmonizes. This is one of the secrets behind Streamline Modern. Before adding any new designs, we make sure they will blend decoratively."

Heywood-Wakefield's "modern" furniture from the 1930s through World War II is characterized by the aerodynamic Streamline style that was also reflected in the architecture, industrial design, transportation, and other design aspects of that era. "Not only were cars, trains, and ocean liners streamlined for aerodynamic purposes, but the style was applied to furniture, appliances, typography, graphics, jewelry, and fashion as well," observes author and historian Elizabeth McMillian. "Streamlining represented modernity, economy, and efficiency, in addition to aerodynamics. It directed greater awareness of space and sculptural form. Streamlining came to symbolize progress and the shape of a better future …" (2004, 28).

Heywood-Wakefield first employed the term "Streamline" in the title of its 1936 catalog, although the influence of this style can be seen in earlier catalogs as well. This *Streamline Maple* line from 1936 includes furniture made from both maple and birch (though maple was subsequently dropped and birch used almost exclusively for later pieces), as well as a section on upholstered furniture with pieces designed by Gilbert Rhode, Russel Wright, and Leo Jiranek.

By 1939, Heywood-Wakefield was using the term "Streamline Modern" to describe its furniture offerings—which were typified by clean simple lines, rounded edges, and graceful curves—often achieved through the company's signature process of "steam bending" the wood. Later catalogs used either "Streamline Modern" or just "Modern" to advertise what had become a hugely popular and ever-expanding line of furniture for the living room, dining room, and bedroom. The advent of World War II, however, brought with it a sharp decline in this expansion, as more than half of the company's production capacity became targeted towards contracts for war

work. In 1943, offerings were limited to what the company called the "Basic Line of Streamlined Modern Furniture" (changed to the "Revised Basic Line" in 1944, to comply with government regulations regarding the number of patterns that could be made). Despite significantly reducing the number of items available and focusing on those "which lend themselves to efficiency in production," the company still made sure that a well-rounded assortment of furniture for all household rooms was included in the "Basic Line."

Following the war, Heywood-Wakefield gradually returned to its former levels of furniture production, which included not only Modern but expanded lines of its "Old Colony" (Early American style furniture) as well. As the 1940s came to a close, the prewar streamlined designs began evolving into what we now view as a classic 1950s style, marketed simply as "Modern" by Heywood-Wakefield.

The year 1949 saw the introduction of Encore, one of Modern's most well-known and successful postwar lines. As noted by authors Steve and Roger Rouland, Encore's "basic design—solid wood drawer pulls extending almost the entire length of the drawer at the top edge—became one of Modern's most enduring styles of the postwar years. The Encore bedroom group and its companion pieces from the dining and living room became a staple for Heywood-Wakefield, and also lasted until Modern itself was discontinued." (1995, 33) Like their prewar predecessors, Heywood-Wakefield's Modern pieces of the early 1950s were characterized by sleek lines with softly rounded or curved edges. Several lines from the second half of the 1950s digressed somewhat from this "tried and true" look, however, introducing a little more of an angular appearance to the later versions of Heywood's Modern.

Steam Bending
at Heywood-Wakefield

Steam bending of wood was an integral part of Heywood-Wakefield's furniture design and production, used extensively with Modern as well as with several other lines. Company literature proudly notes that Heywood-Wakefield pioneered this process in America and that its hand bending operations had been fully operational by the middle of the nineteenth century. By the 1950s, the "bending room" was turning out thousands of bent parts daily to keep up with the high volume of furniture construction at the plant.

The bending process began with dry stock, which was placed into machines called steam retorts. Inside, live steam saturated the wood until it was actually flexible enough to bend without snapping. Once the bending room crew determined that the wood had been saturated to the correct degree, the now pliable stock was removed from the steam retorts and bent into desired shapes either by hand or machine (hydraulic presses). Drying ovens—where the bent wood was placed for anywhere from four to twenty-four hours—comprised the last step in the process. The drying ovens removed excess moisture from the wood, thereby "setting" the bend so it would retain its new shape indefinitely.

This vintage photograph from 1951 shows a bending room worker checking wood in the steam retorts to see if the correct level of saturation has been reached.

Hand bending a table boxing used on one of the tables in the Modern line.

Catalog copy throughout the lifespan of Modern furniture production stressed quality of construction, scale of size (i.e., pieces were suitable for apartments and cottages as well as larger homes), and versatility. Many pieces could be used in more than one room and for more than one purpose. For example, the M 199 G Console Extension Table (see page 141) was described as "an outstanding example of sensible flexibility. Made so that it can accommodate up to six persons comfortably, it is useful as a console table or a server base as well." Similarly, the C 3312 Hutch Shelf could be used in the dining room atop a server or chest to display china (see page 120) or in the living room as a bookcase (see pages 24 and 29). Other examples include a bedroom vanity serving double-duty as a desk in the living or dining room, a server used as a storage cabinet in the bedroom, an occasional table placed next to the bed as a night stand.

For consumers, the company noted that such functionalism was made possible because "the design of all pieces blends together in character." For its sales force, the company also emphasized the marketing advantage of this versatility: "Be sure to point out to your customers the many dual-purpose pieces in Heywood Modern Furniture," the 1941-42 catalog advises. "Ofttimes, one of these distinctive designs will adapt itself to *many* different rooms and living needs. The tea table [C 3705 G] is swell for small dinettes; for combination living-dining rooms; for game rooms. The gate-leg [C 3957 G] is a smart 'spot' piece for any room … The drop-leaf extension [C 3958 G] is another piece that doubles your sales chances because of its practical, dual-purpose design."

Despite the popularity and high quality of Heywood-Wakefield furniture, the company began experiencing financial woes in the 1960s. While the long-running Modern line was essentially phased out by the early 1960s, the company continued to produce other styles of furniture—including some in the Danish Modern genre as well as some institutional lines—ultimately closing its doors in the late 1970s. It left behind a legacy of smartly designed, well-constructed furniture that captured the fancy of countless homeowners then, and continues to entice collectors, dealers, and furniture lovers now.

Preserved in the company's original catalogs are invaluable photographs and descriptions of Heywood-Wakefield's pro-lific furniture offerings. Reproduced here through the generous cooperation of the Levi Heywood Memorial Library in Gardner, Massachusetts, the catalogs that comprise this book illustrate Heywood-Wakefield's celebrated Streamline Modern and Modern lines, unquestionably the most recognizable and most popular of its furniture through the years. Collectors, designers, and aficionados of vintage furniture will welcome this timeless presentation and valuable resource.

Organization of This Book

All of the images shown in this book are from original Heywood-Wakefield catalogs and other company publications. Organized according to major living areas (living rooms, dining rooms, and bedrooms), these invaluable and historic catalog images take readers on a tour of Heywood-Wakefield's "modern" furnished homes from the 1930s to the 1950s. While some of the earliest images predate the start of what is typically considered the "blond" furniture from Heywood-Wakefield, they are included here to show the evolution of style and form, as well as for general interest.

The earlier catalogs (from the 1930s and 1940s) primarily used photographs of whole room settings to illustrate the various pieces of furniture and how they could be used throughout a home. By the 1950s, Heywood-Wakefield was relying less on such whole room photographs and more on

While Modern furniture was sold primarily for use in private homes, many pieces were sold on a contract basis to hospitals, colleges, retail stores, motels and hotels, etc. *Shop News*, the company's employee newsletter, reported in October 1954 that Heywood-Wakefield Modern was even being used on a tanker, the *W. Alton Jones*. Rooms furnished on the tanker with Modern furniture included the owner's suite, captain's office, and captain's lounge. The picture above is from the March 1954 *Shop News* and shows the Music Room at Louisiana College—completely furnished with Heywood-Wakefield Modern.

pictures of individual items. For ease of organization, therefore, each of the major sections in this book (i.e., living rooms, dining rooms, and bedrooms) has been divided into two subsections—one identified as the Streamline years and covering the 1930s and 1940s, the other identified as the Modern years and covering the 1950s. (This nomenclature is somewhat artificial, of course, as the terms do not really divide quite so neatly by decades and were at times used interchangeably, but serves the purpose of separating the two overall types of images.) Within the Modern years sections, the individual images have been further broken down by type of item (e.g., Upholstered Chairs, Occasional Tables, Dining Chairs, etc.).

Some of the earlier items (i.e., those from the 1930s and 1940s) may appear more than once in this book, as they were often featured in multiple room settings within the catalogs. Given space considerations, most of the 1950s pieces are shown here only once, however, even if they could be used in different ways or in different rooms.

The descriptions accompanying each image have been transcribed from original catalog copy or price lists. Included are model numbers, item names, measurements, finishes available (where originally included with descriptions), and any pertinent information regarding style or function. (Slight variations in caption format reflect the years spanned by catalog material.) Yardage required for upholstered pieces, shipping weights, and other extraneous catalog copy was excluded. Editorial comments of interest to readers have been added in italics to differentiate them from original company comments, if any. Further detail on the finishes used by Heywood-Wakefield can be found in the Appendix, pages 237-238.

Dates of production (shown in parentheses with each item) were added for the purposes of this book and obviously did not appear in the original catalogs. Note that dates are based on catalog publication dates (sometimes only estimated) and may not reflect the actual time that pieces were available. In addition, some catalog documentation may be missing. Dates should therefore be considered approximate, though in most cases any disparity would most likely involve only one or two years on either side of the range provided.

The current values provided for each item represent a guideline only and are intended to provide readers with a general idea of what they might expect to pay for each piece in today's market. The values shown reflect these items in excellent, near-mint condition. It is entirely possible to purchase an item for a higher or lower amount than the value shown here, as many factors affect the actual price paid. These factors include condition, scarcity, the venue of the market, and the buyer's relative desire to own a particular item.

The Heywood-Wakefield Plant at Gardner, Massachusetts

houses the general offices and the manufacturing facilities for Modern and Old Colony furniture, Ashcraft furniture, Baby Carriages, Railway Car and Bus seating.

The Orillia, Ontario, Canada plant, produces Baby Carriages, Doll Carriages, and chromium plated furniture for Canadian distribution.

The Lloyd Manufacturing Company plant at Menominee, Michigan manufactures chromium plated furniture for household and outdoor use, Reception Room furniture, Theatre Seating and School furniture.

At our Los Angeles plant many of the products manufactured at Gardner are assembled and finished. There, also, a line of upholstered goods is made for West Coast use.

At the height of its production, Heywood-Wakefield operated four separate plants. These company photographs illustrate the primary plant, located in Gardner, Massachusetts, along with three additional plant locations in Canada, Michigan, and California.

Living Rooms

Our "tour" of the Heywood-Wakefield furnished home begins with the living room, and features upholstered seating, occasional tables, desks, bookcases, and utility cases. Early upholstered pieces sometimes featured unusual maple panel ends (see page 16), while many others through the years used wood trim on the front or sides to "break up" the otherwise all fabric appearance. Desks and bookcases could of course be found in other rooms of the home, but are included here as they appeared in many of the living room settings from the early catalogs.

In company literature, Heywood-Wakefield notes that it was "among the first to develop the sectional sofa idea on a reasonably priced, volume scale." Sectionals were promoted as a way to obtain practical, flexible seating—a "custom-built look" without major expense—and comprised a significant portion of Heywood-Wakefield's furniture offerings from the 1930s forward.

1930s and 1940s – The Streamline Years

C 2601 C – Bentwood Arm Chair (1935) Seat 19" x 18". Height of back 17". *Finish—* Walma. ($550-650)

C 2682 – Hanging Bookcase or Utility Cabinet (1935) Woods—Quilted Maple and Plain Striped Walnut. Fitted with sliding door. Case is shipped with hangers. It may also be used on top of the C 2681 cabinets. Length 48". Width 9". Height 20". *Finish—* Walma. ($700-800)

C 2681 – Two Section Utility Case (1935) Fitted with sliding door. This door may be lifted and fastened in horizontal position for serving and writing. Length 48". Width 15". Height 36". *Exterior finish—*Walma. Interior, adjustable shelves, and back in Cork finish. ($1,000-1,200)

C 2690 LR – Leg Rest (1935) Top 22" x 22". Height 15". ($400-500)

C 2697 C – Chromium Frame Arm Chair (1935) Width of seat 17 ½". Depth of seat 23". Height of back 16". ($900-1,000)

C 2693 – Left Arm Chair (1935) Width of seat 20". Depth of seat 23". Height of back 16". ($500-600)

C 2674 G – Round Front Corner Table (1935) Fitted with two-way drawer and deep storage drawer. Woods—Quilted Maple and Plain Striped Walnut. Top 26 ¾" x 26 ¾". Height 15 7/8". *Finish—*Walma. ($800-900)

C 2692 – Center or Armless Love Seat (1935) Width of seat 40". Depth of seat 23". Height of back 16". ($1,000-1,200)

C 2691 – Right Arm Chair (1935) Width of seat 20". Depth of seat 23". Height of back 16". ($500-600)

C 2682 – Hanging Bookcase or Utility Cabinet (1935) Woods—Quilted Maple and Plain Striped Walnut. Fitted with sliding door. Case is shipped with hangers. It may also be used on top of the C 2681 cabinets. Length 48". Width 9". Height 20". *Finish*—Walma. ($700-800)

C 2695 C – Reading Chair (1935) Width of seat 21". Depth of seat 22". Height of back 22". ($1,200-1,500)

C 2681 – Two Section Utility Case (1935) Fitted with sliding door. This door may be lifted and fastened in horizontal position for serving and writing. Length 48". Width 15". Height 36". *Exterior finish*—Walma. Interior, adjustable shelves, and back in Cork finish. ($1,000-1,200)

C 2601 A – Bentwood Side Chair (1935) Seat 16" x 14 ½". Height of back 17". *Finish*—Walma. ($400-500)

C 2688 G – Combination Dining and Console Table (1935) Top folds lengthwise to form console table. Size of top open 50" x 46". Folded 50" x 23". Height of table 29". Woods—Quilted Maple and Plain Striped Walnut. *Finish*—Walma. ($1,200-1,500)

C 2675 W – Desk (1935) Fitted with 3 drawers on right hand side. Bottom drawer regulation file cabinet size. Woods—Quilted Maple and Plain Striped Walnut. Size of top 45" x 21 ¾". Height 30". ($1,300-1,500)

C 2694 C – Arm Chair with Concealed Spring Base (1935) The back and seat on this chair recline as one unit due to a concealed spring base in the chair. Width of seat 21". Depth of seat 23". Height of back 19". ($1,200-1,500)

C 2690-60 – Davenport (1935) Width of seat 60". Depth of seat 23". Height of back 18". ($2,000-2,200)

C 2679 G – Glass Top Table (1935) Chromium plated base. Circular top—28" diameter. Height 16". ($800-1,000)

C 2698 C – Cocktail Chair (1935) Width of seat 20". Depth of seat 26". Height of back 16". ($900-1,000)

C 2674 G – Round Front Corner Table (1935) Fitted with two-way drawer and deep storage drawer. Woods—Quilted Maple and Plain Striped Walnut. Top 26 ¾" x 26 ¾". Height 15 7/8". *Finish*—Walma. ($800-900)

C 2690 C – Arm Chair (1935) Width of seat 20". Depth of seat 22". Height of back 19". ($900-1,000)

C 2673 G – Two-Tier Lamp Table (1935) Fitted with drawer—Chromium plated handle pull. Woods—Quilted Maple and Plain Striped Walnut. Length 26". Width 14". Height 26". ($700-800)

13

C 2692 – Center or Armless Love Seat (1935) Width of seat 40". Depth of seat 23". Height of back 16". ($1,000-1,200)

C 2678 G – Glass Top Coffee Table (1935) Chromium plated base. Rectangular top 27 ½" x 16". ($750-850)

C 2674 G – Round Front Corner Table (1935) Fitted with two-way drawer and deep storage drawer. Woods—Quilted Maple and Plain Striped Walnut. Top 26 ¾" x 26 ¾". Height 15 7/8". *Finish*—Walma. ($800-900)

C 2691 – Right Arm Chair (1935) Width of seat 20". Depth of seat 23". Height of back 16". ($500-600)

C 2672 G – Two-Tier Coffee Table (1935-36) Open end space under top tier for magazines, etc. Woods—Quilted Maple and Plain Striped Walnut. Length 30". Width 15". Height 20". *Finish*—Walma. ($550-650)

C 2690 C – Arm Chair (1935) Width of seat 20". Depth of seat 22". Height of back 19". ($900-1,000)

C 2673 G – Two-Tier Lamp Table (1935) Fitted with drawer—Chromium plated handle pull. Woods—Quilted Maple and Plain Striped Walnut. Length 26". Width 14". Height 26". ($700-800)

C 2680 – Bookcase or One-section Utility Case (1935) Woods—Quilted Maple and Plain Striped Walnut. Length 24". Width 15". Height 36". *Exterior finish*—Walma. Interior, adjustable shelves, and back in Cork finish. ($800-900)

C 2787 C – Arm Chair (1936-40) Width of seat 24". Depth of seat 20". Height of back 15". *Available* in Wheat, Champagne, Amber, Bleached, and Modern Walnut. ($750-900)

C 2930-W – Kneehole Desk (1936-37) Fully finished on rear. Size of top 42" x 20". Height 30". *Available* in Amber, Bleached, combination of Amber or Bleached. ($1,150-1,350)

14

C 2920-60 – Davenport
(1936-37) Reversible spring
filled seat and back
cushions. Width of seat 60".
Depth of seat 23". Height of
back 18". *Available* in
Amber and Bleached.
($1,500-1,800)

C 2923 G – Coffee Table
(1936-37) Size of top 30" x
18". Height 17". *Available* in
Amber or Bleached. ($450-
550)

C 2922 G – Corner Table
(1936-38) Top 28" in
diameter. Height 28".
Available in Wheat, Amber,
or Bleached. ($550-650)

C 2912 – Hutch-Shelf
(1936-37) This piece may be
used on the C 2917 Server
to form a dining hutch or on
the C 2911 W to form a
secretary. Size 31" x 11".
Height 24". *Available* in
Amber or Bleached. ($300-
400)

C 2911-W – Desk-Chest
(1936-37) This Desk-chest
may be used alone or
combined with the C 2912
shelf to form a secretary.
Size of top 32" x 19". Height
34". *Available* in Amber,
Bleached, combination of
Amber and Bleached.
($1,100-1,200)

C 2920 C – Arm Chair
(1936-37) Reversible spring
filled back and seat cushions.
Width of seat 22". Depth of
seat 23". Height of back 18".
Available in Amber or
Bleached. ($1,050-1,250)

**C 2929 – Compartment
Bookcase** (1936-38) Fitted
with shelf inside of large,
closed section on left. Length
36". Depth 10 ¾". Height 32
½". *Available* in Wheat,
Amber, or Bleached. ($900-
1,000)

**C 2928 – Open Shelf
Bookcase** (1936-38) Length
36". Depth 10 ¾". Height 32
½". *Available* in Wheat,
Amber, or Bleached. ($650-
750)

**C 2794 ACB – Side Chair
with Channel Back** (1936-38)
Seat 15 ½" x 14 ½". Height of
back 16 ½". Channel type
upholstery on the back.
Available in Wheat, Amber,
Bleached, Modern Walnut.
($650-750)

**C 3170 G – Two-Tier
End Table** (1936-39) Size
of top 27" x 14". Height
21". *Available* in Wheat,
Champagne, Amber, and
Bleached. ($450-550)

C 3172-63 – Davenport
(1936-37) Width of seat
63". Depth of seat 22".
Height of back 22".
Available in Amber or
Bleached. ($1,500-1,800)

C 3171 G – Coffee Table
(1936-38) Size of top 34"
x 16". Height 15".
Available in Wheat,
Amber, or Bleached.
($500-600)

**C 2929 – Compartment
Bookcase** (1936-38)
Fitted with shelf inside of
large, closed section on
left. Length 36". Depth
10 ¾". Height 32 ½".
Available in Wheat,
Amber, or Bleached.
($900-1,000)

C 3172 C – Arm Chair
(1936-37) Width of seat
22". Depth of seat 22".
Height of back 22".
($1,000-1,200)
Available in Amber or
Bleached.

C 3173-66 – Davenport
(1936-37) Width of seat 66".
Depth of seat 24". Height of
back 22". *Available* in Amber,
Walnut, or Bleached. ($2,000-
2,200)

C 2921 G – Coffee Table
(1936-39) Top 28" in diameter.
Height 17". *Available* in
Wheat, Champagne, Amber,
and Bleached. ($650-750)

C 3173 C – Arm Chair (1936-
37) Width of seat 21". Depth
of seat 24". Height of back
22". *Available* in Amber,
Walnut, or Bleached. ($1,200-
1,500)

C 2927 G – End Table (1936-
38) Size of top 26" x 11".
Height 21". *Available* in
Wheat, Amber, or Bleached.
($450-550)

C 2926 G – End/Chairside Table
(1936-37) Size of top 26" x 12".
Height 21". *Available* in Amber or
Bleached. ($450-550)

C 3174-66 – Davenport (1936-37)
Width of seat 66". Depth of seat
24". Height of back 21". *Available*
in Amber, Walnut, or Bleached.
($1,250-1,500)

C 2924 G – Coffee Table (1936-
37) Size of top 24" x 19". Height
17". *Available* in Amber or
Bleached. ($250-350)

**C 2925 G – Console or Game
Table** (1936-38) The top of this
table folds and pivots. It serves as a
small wall table; as a console table;
or, with the top turned, as a game
table. Size of top open 32" square;
folded 32" x 16". Height 28".
Available in Wheat, Amber, or
Bleached. ($900-1,000)

C 3174 C – Arm Chair (1936-37)
Width of seat 21". Depth of seat
24". Height of back 21". *Available*
in Amber, Walnut, or Bleached.
($650-750)

In their 1936 catalog, Heywood-Wakefield notes that the
upholstered furniture and occasional tables shown in the next
seven photographs were primarily the works of leading styl-
ist-designers such as Gilbert Rhode, Russel Wright, Leo
Jiranek, and others. The company characterized these designs as "conservative, effective [and] well tailored ... adaptable to good modern decoration," noting also that the occasional tables were finished in Modern Walnut.

C 2706 G – **End Table** (1936) Wood—Plain
Striped Walnut. Size of top 26" x 13". Height 19
½". *Finish*—Modern Walnut. ($550-650)

C 2790 – **Armless or Center Chair** (1936-37)
Width of seat 21". Depth of seat 24". Height of
back 18". ($650-750)

C 2790 RC – **Right Arm Chair** (1936-37)
Same as above except with right arm. ($600-
700)

C 2790 LC – **Left Arm Chair** (1936-37) Same
as above except with left arm. ($650-750)

C 2792 C – Studio Chair (1936-37) Width of seat 19 ½". Depth of seat 21". Height of back 18". ($700-800)

C 2708 G – Round Front Corner Table (1936) Wood—Plain Striped Walnut. Size of top 26 ½" square. Height 20 ½". *Finish*—Modern Walnut. ($550-650)

C 2791-50 – Love Seat (1936-37) Width of seat 40". Depth of seat 24". Height of back 18". ($1,100-1,500)

C 2690-66 – Davenport (1936) *Shown as discontinued in price list for this catalog.* ($1,800-2,000)

C 2703 G – Coffee Table (1936-37) Wood—Plain Striped Walnut. Size of top 27 ½" x 18". Height 17". *Finish*—Modern Walnut. ($700-800)

C 2690 C – Arm Chair (1935) Width of seat 20". Depth of seat 22". Height of back 19". ($900-1,000)

C 2672 G – Two-Tier Coffee Table (1935-36) Open end space under top tier for magazines, etc. Woods— Quilted Maple and Plain Striped Walnut. Length 30". Width 15". Height 20". *Finish*—Walma. ($550-650)

C 2698 C – Cocktail Chair (1935) Width of seat 20". Depth of seat 26". Height of back 16". ($900-1,000)

C 2705 G – Coffee Table (1936-37) Wood—Plain Striped Walnut. Size of top 27 ½" in diameter. Height 17". *Finish*—Modern Walnut. ($700-800)

C 2698-66 – Davenport (1936-37) Width of seat 66". Depth of seat 24". Height of back 17". ($1,800-2,000)

C 2789 C – Arm Chair (1936-37) Width of seat 20 ½". Depth of seat 23". Height of back 19". ($800-900)

C 2704 G – Coffee Table (1936-37) Wood—Plain Striped Walnut. Size of top 36" x 18". Height 17". *Finish*—Modern Walnut. ($750-850)

C 2789-66 – Davenport (1936-37) Width of seat 66". Depth of seat 23". Height of back 19". ($1,200-1,500)

19

C 2707 G – Two-Tier Lamp Table (1936-37) Wood—Plain Striped Walnut. Size on top 28" x 13". Height 24". *Finish—* Modern Walnut. ($500-600)

C 2778-60 – Davenport (1936) Width of seat 60". Depth of seat 22". Height of back 19". ($1,200-1,500)

C 2670 G – Coffee Table (1935-36) Woods—Yuba and Plain Striped Walnut. Size of top 30" x 17". Height 16". *Finish—* Modern Walnut. ($700-800)

C 2778 C – Arm Chair (1936) Width of seat 20". Depth of seat 22". Height of back 19". ($700-800)

C 2671 G – Two-Tier Lamp Table (1935-36) Fitted with two-way drawer which opens from either side. Woods—Yuba and Plain Striped Walnut. Size of top 32" x 16 ½". Height 19 ¼". *Finish—* Modern Walnut. ($500-600)

C 2781 C – Arm Chair (1936) Width of seat 21". Depth of seat 24". Height of back 19". ($1,000-1,100)

C 2788 C – Arm Chair (1936-37) Width of seat 20". Depth of seat 23". Height of back 19". ($900-1,000)

C 2706 G – End Table (1936) Wood—Plain Striped Walnut. Size of top 26" x 13". Height 19 ½". *Finish—* Modern Walnut. ($550-650)

C 2786 C – Arm Chair (1936-37) Width of seat 20". Depth of seat 19". Height of back 18". *Available* in Amber, Bleached or Modern Walnut. ($600-700)

C 3166 – Dressing Table (1936-37) Size of top 34" x 17". Height 30". *Available* in Amber, Bleached, combination of Amber and Bleached. ($650-800)

C 3175 C – Barrel Chair (1936-37) Width of seat 23". Depth of seat 23". Height of back 19". *Available* in Amber or Bleached. ($850-1,050)

C 2785 C – Sleepy Hollow Chair (1936-37) Width of seat 23". Depth of seat 23". Height of back 29 ½". ($800-900)

C 2794 C – Arm Chair (1936-40) Seat 19" x 17". Height of back 17". *Available* in Wheat, Champagne, Amber, Bleached, or Modern Walnut. ($650-750)

C 2794 A – Side Chair (1936) Seat 15 ½" x 14 ½". Height of back 16 ½". *Available* in Wheat, Champagne, Amber, Bleached, or Modern Walnut. ($550-650)

C 2925 G – Console or Game Table (1936-38) The top of this table folds and pivots. It serves as a small wall table; as a console table; or, with the top turned, as a game table. Size of top open 32" square; folded 32" x 16". Height 28". *Available* in Wheat, Amber, or Bleached. ($900-1,000)

C 2687 A – Side Chair (1935-37) This is the chair shown against the wall. Seat 18" x 16 ½". Height of back 15". *Available* in Walma, Amber, Bleached, Modern Walnut. ($450-550)

C 3343-66 – Davenport
(1937-38) Width of seat 66". Depth of seat 23". Height of back 21". *Available* in Wheat, Amber, or Bleached. ($2,500-2,900)

C 3341 C – Arm Chair
(1937-38) Width of seat 22". Depth of seat 23". Height of back 21". *Available* in Wheat, Amber, or Bleached. ($1,000-1,200)

C 3327 G – Corner Table
(1937-38) Size of top 32 ½" square. Height 22". *Available* in Wheat, Amber, or Bleached. ($650-750)

C 2921 G – Coffee Table
(1936-39) Top 28" in diameter. Height 17". *Available* in Wheat, Champagne, Amber, and Bleached. ($650-750)

C 3342-44 – Love Seat
(1937-38) Width of seat 44". Depth of seat 23". Height of back 21". *Available* in Wheat, Amber, or Bleached. ($1,500-1,800)

C 3326 C – Barrel Chair
(1937-39) Seat 23" x 22". Height of back 18 ½". *Available* in Wheat, Champagne, Amber, Bleached, or Modern Walnut. ($750-850)

C 3170 G – Two-Tier End Table (1936-39) Size of top 27" x 14". Height 21". *Available* in Wheat, Champagne, Amber, and Bleached. ($450-550)

C 2927 G – End Table
(1936-38) Size of top 26" x 11". Height 21". *Available* in Wheat, Amber, or Bleached. ($450-550)

C 3341 – Single Filler or Armless Center Section
(1937-38) Width of seat 22". Depth of seat 23". Height of back 21". *Available* in Wheat, Amber, or Bleached. ($400-500)

C 3341 RC – Right Arm Chair (1937-38) Same as above except with right arm only. ($500-600)

C 3341 LC – Left Arm Chair (1937-38) Same as above except with left arm only. ($500-600)

C 3327 G – Corner Table
(1937-38) Size of top 32 ½" square. Height 22". *Available* in Wheat, Amber, or Bleached. ($650-750)

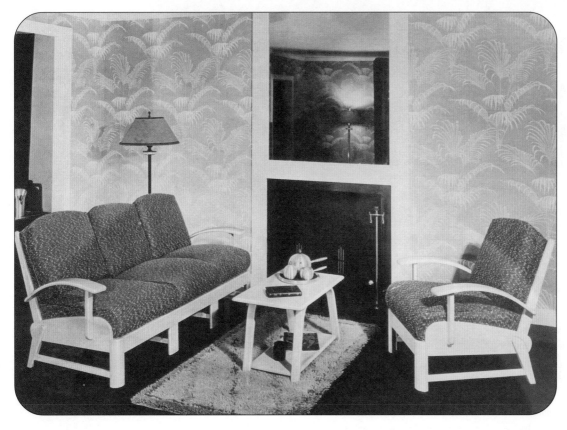

C 3344-63 – Davenport
(1937) Width of seat 63". Depth of seat 23". Height of back 19". ($1,500-1,800)

C 3344 C – Arm Chair
(1937) Width of seat 23". Depth of seat 23". Height of back 19". ($800-900)

C 3367-66 – Davenport (1938-39) Width of seat 66". Depth of seat 21". Height of back 19". *Available* in Wheat, Champagne, Amber, or Bleached. *Designed by Alfons Bach.* ($4,500-5,000)

C 3367 C – Arm Chair (1938-39) Width of seat 22". Depth of seat 20". Height of back 20". *Available* in Wheat, Champagne, Amber, or Bleached. *Designed by Alfons Bach.* ($2,200-2,500)

C 3170 G – Two-Tier End Table (1936-39) Size of top 27" x 14". Height 21". *Available* in Wheat, Champagne, Amber, and Bleached. ($450-550)

C 3348 – Corner Cabinet (1938-39) Equally adaptable to the dining room or the living room of the modern home. It measures 14 ½" deep; 24" wide; and 65" high. Lower closed compartment fitted with shelf. *Available* in Wheat, Champagne, Amber, or Bleached. ($1,200-1,400)

C 3364 G – Cocktail Table (1938) Size of top 34" in diameter. Height 16". *Available* in Wheat, Amber, or Bleached.($600-700)

C 3368-63 – Davenport (1938) Width of seat 63". Depth of seat 23". Height of back 19". *Available* in Wheat, Amber, or Bleached. ($3,000-3,500)

C 3368 C – Arm Chair (1938) Width of seat 22". Depth of seat 22". Height of back 19". *Available* in Wheat, Amber, or Bleached. ($1,500-2,000)

C 3345 G – Lamp Table (1938) Size of top 22" x 22". Height 26". *Available* in Wheat, Amber, or Bleached. ($450-550)

C 3312 – Hutch-Shelf (1937-39) This piece may be used with the C 3310 chest to form an open shelf hutch buffet; with the C 3311 W Desk-Chest to form a Secretary Desk; or with the C 3314 Server to form a dining hutch. Size 31" x 11". Height 25". *Available* in Wheat, Champagne, Amber, or Bleached. ($400-500)

C 3311 W – Desk-Chest (1937-39) This Desk-Chest may be used alone or combined with the C 3312 shelf to form a secretary. Size of top 32" x 19". Height 34". *Available* in Wheat, Champagne, Amber, or Bleached. ($800-950)

C 2794 A 4CB – Channel Back Side Chair (1938-40) Seat 15 ½" x 14 ½". Height of back 16 ½". Upholstered with four channels on back. *Available* in Wheat, Champagne, Amber, Bleached, or Modern Walnut. ($650-750)

C 3383 C – Cane Panel Arm Chair (1938) Seat 20" x 23". Height of back 16". *Available* in Wheat. ($500-600)

C 2922 G – Corner Table (1936-38) Top 28" in diameter. Height 28". *Available* in Wheat, Amber, or Bleached. ($550-650)

C 3368 R – Wood Frame Arm Chair (1938) Width of seat 22 ½". Depth of seat 23". Height of back 24". *Available* in Wheat, Amber, or Bleached. ($800-900)

C 3365 A – Cane Back Side Chair (1938) Seat 15 ½" x 14 ½". Height of back 16 ½". *Available* in Wheat. ($350-400)

C 3328 W – Kneehole Desk (1937-39) Fully finished including rear. Size of top 42" x 20". Height 30". *Available* in Wheat, Champagne, Amber, or Bleached. ($1,150-1,350)

C 2927 G – End Table (1936-38) Size of top 26" x 11". Height 21". *Available* in Wheat, Amber, or Bleached. ($450-550)

C 3387 C – Arm Chair (1938-40) Reversible seat cushion. Width of seat 24". Depth of seat 22". Height of back 23". *Available* in Wheat, Champagne, Amber, Bleached, or Modern Walnut. ($1,250-1,500)

C 3349 G – Gate-Leg Table (1938-40) A popular Gate-leg Dining Table with a multitude of uses in the modern home. The top measures 36" x 60" with both drop leaves extended. With one leaf up, it is 36" square. With both leaves down, the top measures 36" x 13 ¾" and may readily serve as a console, wall or ball table. Height 29". *Available* in Wheat, Champagne, Amber, or Bleached. ($650-850)

C 3386 C – Full-Upholstered Arm Chair (1938-39) Width of seat 18". Depth of seat 18". Height of back 17". *Available* in Wheat, Champagne, Amber, Bleached, or Modern Walnut. ($1,250-1,400)

C 3366 W – Desk-Chest-Bookcase (1938-39) An ideal piece for the modern home…compact and with a multitude of uses. Length 48". Depth 12". Height 48". *Available* in Wheat, Champagne, Amber, or Bleached. ($1,500-1,800)

C 3385 C – Open Side Arm Chair (1938-39) Width of seat 19". Depth of seat 20". Height of back 17". *Available* in Wheat, Champagne, Amber, Bleached, or Modern Walnut. ($500-600)

C 3381 C – Cane Panel Arm Chair (1938-40) Width of seat 20". Depth of seat 23". Height of back 16". *Available* in Wheat. ($500-600)

C 2925 G – Console or Game Table (1936-38) The top of this table folds and pivots. It serves as a small wall table; as a console table; or, with the top turned, as a game table. Size of top open 32" square; folded 32" x 16". Height 28". *Available* in Wheat, Amber, or Bleached. ($900-1,000)

C 3388 C – Upholstered Arm Chair (1938-39) Width of seat 19 ½". Depth of seat 20 ½". Height of back 14". *Available* in Wheat, Champagne, Amber, Bleached, or Modern Walnut. ($900-1,000)

Described in the catalog as "Swedish Modern," these two chairs could be used not only in living rooms, but also in offices, cocktail lounges, etc. Wheat was the recommended finish, as it best complemented the woven cane.

C 3384 C – Oval Panel Cane Chair (1938-39) Reversible seat cushion. Width of seat 20 ½". Depth of seat 22". Height of back 18". *Available* in Wheat. ($650-750)

C 3364 G – Cocktail Table (1938) Size of top 34" in diameter. Height 16". *Available* in Wheat, Amber, or Bleached. ($600-700)

C 3382 C – Squared Panel Arm Chair (1938-39) Width of seat 20". Depth of seat 22". Height of back 18". *Available* in Wheat. ($500-600)

C 3538 G – Side Extension Table (1939) Size of top closed 20" x 50". Top open 30" x 50". Fitted with one leaf. Height 29". *Available* in Wheat, Champagne, Amber, or Bleached. ($1,000-1,150)

C 3526 A – Side Chair (1939-40) Seat 15 ½" x 14 ½". Height of back 16 ½". *Available* in Wheat, Champagne, Amber or Bleached. ($450-500)

C 3387 C – Arm Chair (1938-40) Reversible seat cushion. Width of seat 24". Depth of seat 22". Height of back 23". *Available* in Wheat, Champagne, Amber, Bleached, or Modern Walnut. ($1,250-1,500)

C 3531 G – End Table (1939) Top 13 ½" x 26 ¼". Height 20 ½". *Available* in Wheat, Champagne, Amber or Bleached. ($250-350)

The sectional pieces in this grouping were designed by Count Alexis de Sakhnoffsky.

C 3170 G – Two-Tier End Table (1936-39) Size of top 27" x 14". Height 21". *Available* in Wheat, Champagne, Amber, and Bleached. ($450-550)

C 3541 – Single Filler (1939-40) Width of seat 22". Depth of seat 24". Height of back 18". Reversible seat cushion. ($400-500)

C 3541 RC – Right Arm Chair (1939-40) Same as above except with right arm only. ($500-600)

C 3541 LC – Left Arm Chair (1939-40) Same as above except with left arm only. ($500-600)

C 3542 – Double Filler (1939-40) Width of seat 44". Depth of seat 24". Height of back 18". Reversible seat cushions (not shown). ($500-600)

C 3540 G – Corner Table (1939-40) Size of top 31 ½" square. Height 22". *Available* in Wheat, Champagne, Amber, or Bleached. ($800-900)

C 3548 G – Round Cocktail Table (1939-40) Fitted with revolving top which measures 32" in diameter. Height 16". *Available* in Wheat, Champagne, Amber, or Bleached. ($500-600)

A complete ensemble designed by Count Sakhnoffsky.

C 3543-66 – Davenport (1939-40) Width of seat 66". Depth of seat 24". Height of back 17". Reversible seat cushions. *Available* in Wheat, Champagne, Amber, or Bleached. ($1,850-2,200)

C 3541 C – Arm Chair (1939-40) Width of seat 21". Depth of seat 24". Height of back 18". Reversible seat cushion. *Available* in Wheat, Champagne, Amber, or Bleached. ($1,050-1,200)

C 3546 G – End Table (1939-40) Top 28" x 15". Height 22". Fitted with shelf. *Available* in Wheat, Champagne, Amber, or Bleached. ($750-900)

C 3547 G – Cocktail Table (1939-40) Top 36" x 19". Height 16". Fitted with shelf. *Available* in Wheat, Champagne, Amber, or Bleached. ($1,000-1,200)

C 3549 G – Lamp Table (1939-42) Fitted with shelf. Top 22" in diameter. Height 26". *Available* in Wheat, Champagne, Amber, or Bleached. ($550-650)

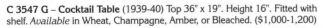

The davenport, chair, coffee table, and lamp table in this grouping were designed by Alfons Bach.

C 3579-63 – Davenport (1939) Width of seat 63". Depth of seat 23". Height of back 20". *Available* in Wheat, Champagne, Amber, or Bleached. ($2,500-3,000)

C 3579 C – Arm Chair (1939) Width of seat 21 ½". Depth of seat 23". Height of back 19". *Available* in Wheat, Champagne, Amber, or Bleached. ($1,250-1,500)

C 3532 G – Coffee Table (1939) Top 19" x 37". Height 16 ½". *Available* in Wheat, Champagne, Amber, or Bleached. ($250-350)

C 3170 G – Two-Tier End Table (1936-39) Size of top 27" x 14". Height 21". *Available* in Wheat, Champagne, Amber, and Bleached. ($450-550)

C 3533 G – Lamp Table (1939) Top 17" x 19". Height 28". *Available* in Wheat, Champagne, Amber, and Bleached. ($150-200)

C 3521 R – Barrel Chair (1939) Reversible seat cushion. Width of seat 27 ½". Depth of seat 22". Height of back 19 ½". *Available* in Wheat, Champagne, Amber, or Bleached. ($650-750)

C 3312 – Hutch-Shelf (1937-39) This piece may be used with the C 3310 chest to form an open shelf hutch buffet; with the C 3311 W Desk-Chest to form a Secretary Desk; or with the C 3314 Server to form a dining hutch. Size 31" x 11". Height 25". *Available* in Wheat, Champagne, Amber, or Bleached. ($400-500)

C 3311 W – Desk-Chest (1937-39) This Desk-Chest may be used alone or combined with the C 3312 shelf to form a secretary. Size of top 32" x 19". Height 34". *Available* in Wheat, Champagne, Amber, or Bleached. ($800-950)

C 3535 A – Side Chair (1939-43) Seat 16" x 16 ½". Height of back 17". *Available* in Wheat, Champagne, Amber, or Bleached. ($375-475)

C 3535 C – Arm Chair
(1939-43) Width between arms 17 ½". Depth of seat 16 ½". Height of back 17". *Available* in Wheat, Champagne, Amber, or Bleached. ($450-550)

C 3539 W – Vanity Base or Kneehole Desk (1939-40) Size of top 48" x 21". Height 30". Fully finished including rear. *Available* in Wheat, Champagne, Amber, or Bleached. ($1,850-2,150)

C 3326 C – Barrel Chair (1937-39) Seat 23" x 22". Height of back 18 ½". *Available* in Wheat, Champagne, Amber, Bleached, or Modern Walnut. ($750-850)

C 3534 – Bookcase (1939) Top 12 ½" x 41". Height 29 ¼". *Available* in Wheat, Champagne, Amber, or Bleached. ($350-450)

C 3381 C – Cane Panel Arm Chair (1938-40) Width of seat 20". Depth of seat 23". Height of back 16". *Available* in Wheat. $500-600)

C 3545 – Sectional Bookcase (1939-40) Fitted with adjustable shelves. Top 36" x 11". Height 22". *Available* in Wheat, Champagne, Amber, or Bleached. ($650-750)

C 3544 – Pier Cabinet (1939-40) Top 16" x 14". Height 32 ½". *Available* in Wheat, Champagne, Amber, or Bleached. ($850-1,000)

C 3328 W – Kneehole Desk (1937-39) Fully finished including rear. Size of top 42" x 20". Height 30". *Available* in Wheat, Champagne, Amber, or Bleached. ($1,150-1,350)

C 2794 A 4CB – Channel Back Side Chair (1938-40) Seat 15 ½" x 14 ½". Height of back 16 ½". Upholstered with four channels on back. *Available* in Wheat, Champagne, Amber, Bleached, or Modern Walnut. ($650-750)

C 3388 C – Upholstered Arm Chair (1938-39) Width of seat 19 ½". Depth of seat 20 ½". Height of back 14". *Available* in Wheat, Champagne, Amber, Bleached, or Modern Walnut. ($900-1,000)

C 3384 C – Oval Panel Cane Chair (1938-39) Reversible seat cushion. Width of seat 20 ½". Depth of seat 22". Height of back 18". *Available* in Wheat. ($650-750)

C 3389 G – Console or Game Table (1939-42) The top of this table folds and pivots. It serves as a small wall table; as a console table; or, with the top turned, as a game table. Size of top open 32" square; folded 32" x 16". Height 28". *Available* in Wheat, Champagne, Amber, or Bleached. ($950-1,000)

C 3382 C – Squared Panel Arm Chair (1938-39) Width of seat 20". Depth of seat 22". Height of back 18". *Available* in Wheat. ($500-600)

In 1939, Heywood-Wakefield published a full size catalog as well as a smaller, brochure-type catalog, the latter designed to illustrate for potential customers the many ways that Heywood furniture could be used throughout the home. Included in this smaller catalog (titled *Streamline Modern by Heywood-Wakefield*) was a "recently introduced" furniture ensemble identified as "Textured Modern." As shown in the catalog, this Textured Modern ensemble (which included the living room pieces shown below as well as dining room and bedroom pieces, shown later) featured an incised chevron motif and was described as: "Definitely smart and definitely Swedish in character … Modern, incisive carvings on solid wood create an entirely original effect which is suggestive of patterned fabric." No other documentation was found for this unusual grouping. While shown in the 1939 brochure, Textured Modern may have been produced only for a very brief time or not at all.

C 3521 R – Barrel Chair (1939) Reversible seat cushion. Width of seat 27 ½". Depth of seat 22". Height of back 19 ½". *Available* in Wheat, Champagne, Amber, or Bleached. ($650-750)

C 3520-63 – Sofa (1939) ($1,200-1,500)

C 3522 G – Coffee Table (1939) Top 17" x 34". ($350-450)

C 3524 G – End Table (1939) ($250-300)

C 3525 – Bookcase (1939) Top 33" x 12". ($450-550)

31

C 3753 G – **End Table** (1940-44) Top 30" x 15". Height 22". ($500-600)

C 3541 RC – **Right Arm Chair** (1939-40) Seat 22" x 24". Height of back 18". Reversible seat cushion. ($500-600)

C 3541 LC – **Left Arm Chair** (1939-40) This is one-arm chair next to fireplace. Same as above except with left arm only. ($500-600)

C 3541 – **Single Filler** (1939-40) This is single size, armless center section. Seat 22" x 24". Height of back 18". Reversible seat cushion. ($400-500)

C 3542 – **Double Filler** (1939-40) Same as single filler except seat is 44" wide (not shown). ($500-600)

C 3540 G – **Corner Table** (1939-40) This is table shown in large view. Size of top 31 ½" square. Height 22". ($800-900)

C 3548 G – **Round Cocktail Table** (1939-40) Fitted with revolving top 32" in diameter. Height 16". ($500-600)

C 3755 G – **Corner Table** (1940-44) This is table shown in small view at left. It may also be used with the sectional sofa if desired. Size of top 29" square. Height 22 ½". ($400-500)

C 3535 A – **Side Chair** (1939-43) Seat 16" x 16 ½". Height of back 17". ($375-475)

C 3539 W – **Vanity Base or Kneehole Desk** (Crescendo) (1939-40) This is a six-drawer Kneehole Desk. The lower left drawer is filing cabinet size. Size of top 48" x 21". Height 30". Fully finished including rear. ($1,850-2,150)

C 3750 G – **Coffee Table** (1940) Size of top 36" x 19". Height 15 ½". ($450-550)

C 3542-44 – **Love Seat** (1939-40) Seat 44" x 24". Height of back 18". *Designed by Count Sakhnoffsky.* ($1,500-1,750)

C 3719 G – **End Table** (1940-42) Fitted with drawer and two shelves. Top 32" x 14". Height 22". ($550-650)

C 3589-66 – Davenport
(1940) Seat 66" x 22".
Height of back 20".
Reversible seat cushions.
($2,150-2,450)

C 3589 C – Arm Chair
(1940) Seat 22" x 22".
Height of back 20".
Reversible seat cushion.
($1,050-1,350)

C 3752 G – End Table
(1940) Top 28" x 14".
Height 21". ($400-500)

**C 3751 G – Cocktail
Table** (1940) Top 30" in
diameter. Height 15". ($550-650)

C 3717 G – Cocktail Table (1940-42) This is table shown in silhouette at right.
Fitted with cigarette and accessory drawer. Size of top 37" x 17". Height 16".
($900-1,050)

C 3762 C – Arm Chair (1940) Seat 23" x 21".
Height of back 21". Built in spring unit—not
reversible. ($1,050-1,200)

C 3763 LR – Leg Rest (1940) Size of top 25" x
21". Height 15". Built in spring unit. ($450-550)

C 3585 – Hutch Top (1940) 30 ½" wide, 24" high, 10 ¼" deep. ($250-400)

C 3584 W – Desk-Chest (1940) 32" wide, 17" deep, 34" high. Top drawer has desk compartment as
shown. Overall height of complete secretary is 58"; overall width, 32". ($1,000-1,100)

C 3764 R – Wing Chair (1940) Seat 18 ½" x 20". Height of back 22". Spring filled seat cushion. Spring
type channel back. ($800-900)

C 3718 G – Cocktail Table (1940-42) This modern Hunt Table (shown at left) is fitted with semi-
circular drawer. Overall measurement of top is 41" x 19". Height 16". ($1,050-1,200)

C 3761-72 – **Davenport** (1940) Seat 72" x 21". Height of back 21". Built in spring unit—not reversible. ($1,850-2,150)

C 3761 C – **Arm Chair** (1940) Seat 23" x 21". Height of back 21". Built in spring unit—not reversible. ($900-1,000)

C 3756 G – **Coffee Table** (1940-43) Top 42" x 20". Height 17". ($550-650)

C 3754 G – **Lamp Table** (1940) Fitted with lower shelf. The clover-leaf top measures 24" in diameter. Height 26 ½". ($400-500)

C 3752 G – **End Table** (1940) Top 28" x 14". Height 21". ($400-500)

C 3760-72 – **Davenport** (1940) Seat 72" x 21". Height of back 21". Built in spring units—not reversible. ($2,250-2,500)

C 3760 C – **Arm Chair** (1940) Seat 23" x 21". Height of back 21". Built in spring unit—not reversible. ($1,250-1,500)

C 3348 X – **Corner Cabinet** (1940-43) This Corner Cabinet is equally adaptable to the living or dining room. It measures 24" wide, 14 ¼" deep, and 65" high. Lower, closed compartment is fitted with shelf. ($1,200-1,400)

C 3750 G – **Coffee Table** (1940) Size of top 36" x 19". Height 15 ½". ($450-550)

C 3752 G – **End Table** (1940) Top 28" x 14". Height 21". ($400-500)

C 3387 C – Arm Chair (1938-40) Seat 24" x 22". Height of back 23". Reversible seat cushion. $1,250-1,500)

C 3544 – Pier Cabinet (1939-40) Fitted with 4 drawers. Size of top 16" x 14". Height 32 ½". ($850-1,000)

C 3582 – Corner Bookcase (1940) This is the open front bookcase in corner of the group shown. Overall measurements are 28" x 28". Height 32 ½". ($800-1,000)

C 3545 – Sectional Bookcase (1939-40) This is the open, straight-front bookcase shown in the group photo. It is fitted with adjustable shelves. Top 36" x 11". Height 32 ½". ($650-750)

C 3583 – Cabinet Base (1940) This is the cabinet bookcase shown in the small view at right. Fitted with 2 storage compartments below. Top 32" wide. Overall depth including swelled front is 13 ¾". Height 32 ½". ($900-1,000)

C 3766 C – Barrel Chair (1940) Seat 22" x 20". Height of back 20". Built in spring units in both seat and vertical channel back. ($650-750)

C 3736 – Vanity Desk (Plaza) (1940) This is a 5-drawer type. Top 44" x 18". Height 30". ($1,250-1,500)

C 3765 C – Arm Chair (1940-42) Seat 22" x 20". Height of back 16". ($750-900)

C 3389 G – Console or Game Table (1939-42) Top of this table folds and pivots. Serves as small wall table; as a console; or, with the top turned, as a card table. Size of top open 32" square, folded 32" x 16". Height 28". ($950-1,000)

C 3349 G – Gate-Leg Table
(1938-40) Dual purpose table for dining or living room. Top measures 36" x 60" with both leaves extended, with one leaf up, it is 36" square. With both leaves down, top measures 36" x 13 ¾". ($650-850)

C 3381 C – Cane Panel Arm Chair (1938-40) Seat 20" x 23". Height of back 16". ($500-600)

C 3586 W – Desk-Chest-Bookcase (1940) A compact unit particularly suited to apartment living rooms. Width 48". Depth 12". Height 44". ($1,550-1,800)

C 3767 C – Reading Chair (1940-42) This is a good man's chair because of its generous proportions. Seat 22" x 22". Height of back 24". Reversible, spring filled seat cushion. Spring filled back. ($1,150-1,250)

The sectional in this grouping was designed by Count Sakhnoffsky.

C 3943 G – End Table (1941-44) Top 28" x 14". Height 22". ($375-475)

C 3945 RC – Right Arm Chair (1941-42) Seat 22" wide, 21" deep. Back 19" high. ($750-850)

C 3945 LC – Left Arm Chair (1941-42) Shown at the right end of the sectional grouping. Same as the C 3945 RC but with left arm only. ($750-850)

C 3945 – Single Filler (1941-42) This is single size, armless center section. Seat 22" x 21" deep. Back is 19" high. (650-750)

C 3946 – Double Filler (1941-42) Same as single filler except seat is 44" wide (not shown). ($800-900)

C 3960 G – Corner Table (1941-42) Shown in large view and also shown separately in small view at left. Top measures 32" square and table is 22" high. ($650-750)

C 3964 G – Cocktail Table (1941-44) Fitted with revolving top. 32" in diameter. Height 17". ($400-500)

All pieces in this grouping were designed by Count Sakhnoffsky.

C 3947-66 – Davenport (1941-42) Seat 66 " x 21". Height of back 19". Reversible seat cushions. ($2,250-2,500)

C 3945 C – Arm Chair (1941-42) Seat 22" x 21". Height of back 19". Reversible seat cushion. ($1,000-1,100)

C 3944 G – Lamp Table (1941-44) Two of these tables are shown flanking the davenport. Size of top 19" x 17". Height 26". ($450-550)

C 3943 G – End Table (1941-44) Shown beside upholstered arm chair. Size of top 28" x 14". Height 22". ($375-475)

C 3942 G – Cocktail Table (1941-44) Size of top 36" x 19". Height 16". ($450-550)

C 3946-44 – Love Seat (1941-42) Seat 44" x 21". Height of back 19". Spring filled, reversible seat cushions. *Designed by Count Sakhnoffsky.* ($1,800-2,000)

C 3948 C – Channel Side Arm Chair (1941-42) Seat measures 28" x 20". Height of back 16". Reversible spring filled seat cushion. ($1,000-1,100)

C 3719 G – End Table (1940-42) This table (shown beside end of love seat) is fitted with single, top drawer and has 2 shelves in addition. Size of top 32" x 14". Height 22". ($550-650)

C 3963 G – Cocktail Table (1941-42) Diameter of top 28". Height 17". ($500-600)

C 3753 G – End Table (1940-44) Top 30" x 15". Height 22". ($500-600)

C 3985 RC – Right Arm Chair (1941-44) Seat 22" x 21". Height of back 19". Reversible seat cushion. ($500-600)

C 3985 LC – Left Arm Chair (1941-44) Shown to the right of the corner table. Same as the C 3985 RC but with left arm only. ($500-600)

C 3985 – Single Filler (1941-44) This is single size, armless center section. Seat measures 22" x 21". Height of back 19". ($400-500)

C 3755 G – Corner Table (1940-44) Top measures 29" square. Height 22 ½". ($400-500)

C 3961 G – Cocktail Table (1941-42) Size of top 36" x 19". Height 16". ($1,000-1,100)

C 3987-66 – Davenport (1941-44) Seat 66" x 21". Back 19" high. Reversible seat cushions. ($2,250-2,500)

C 3985 C – Arm Chair (1941-44) Seat 22" x 21". Back 19" high. Reversible, spring filled seat cushion. ($1,100-1,200)

C 3549 G – Lamp Table (1939-42) Diameter of top 22". Height 26". ($550-650)

C 3717 G – Cocktail Table (1940-42) This practical table is fitted with cigarette and accessory drawer at top. Top measures 36" x 17". Height 16". ($900-1,050)

C 3962 G – End Table (1941-42) Oval top measures 28" x 15". Height 21". ($800-900)

C 3986 – Double Filler (1941-42) This armless, double filler may be used with other sectional pieces or as a separate, armless love seat. Reversible spring filled seat cushions. Seat 44" x 21". Back 19" high. ($1,000-1,200)

C 3978 W – Kneehole Desk (1941-44) This is a six-drawer kneehole desk which is completely finished all around. The lower left drawer is filing cabinet size. Size of top 46" x 21". Height 30". ($1,600-1,800)

C 3535 A – Side Chair (1939-43) Seat 16" x 16 ½". Height of back 17". ($375-475)

C 3961 G – Cocktail Table (1941-42) Top measures 36" x 19". Height 16". ($1,000-1,100)

C 3771 X – End Table (1941-42) Fitted with lower storage compartment with hinged door. It measures 32" x 13". Height 23". ($500-600)

C 3717 G – Cocktail Table (1940-42) This table, shown in small view at right, is fitted with cigarette ($9and accessory drawer. Top measures 36" x 17". Height 16". ($900-1,050)

C 3996 R – Wing Chair (1941-42) Seat 20" x 25". Height of back 22". Spring filled, reversible seat cushion. ($900-1,000)

C 3585 – Hutch Top (1940) 30 ½" wide, 24" high, 10 ¼" deep. ($250-400)

C 3975 W – Desk-Chest (1941-42) 32" wide, 17" deep, 34" high. ($800-900)

C 3767 C – Reading Chair (1940-42) This is a good man's chair because of its generous proportions. Seat 22" x 22". Height of back 24". Reversible, spring filled seat cushion. Spring filled back. ($1,150-1,250)

C 3989-66 – Davenport (1941-42) Seat 66" x 21". Height of back 19". Reversible, spring filled seat cushions. (2,250-2,500)

C 3989 C – Arm Chair (1941-42) Seat 22" x 21". Height of back 19". Reversible, spring filled seat cushions. ($900-1,000)

C 3962 G – End Table (1941-42) Oval top measures 28" x 15". Height 21". ($800-900)

C 3718 G – Cocktail Table (1940-42) Fitted with semi-circular accessory drawer under top of table. Overall measurements of top 41" x 19". Height 16". ($1,050-1,200)

C 3981-68 – Davenport (1941-42) Seat 68" x 21". Height 21". Reversible, spring filled seat cushions. ($2,500-3,000)

C 3981 C – Arm Chair (1941-42) Seat 23" x 21". Height of back 21". Reversible, spring filled seat cushion. ($900-1,000)

C 3753 G – End Table (1940-44) Top 30" x 15". Height 22". ($500-600)

C 3756 G – Coffee Table (1940-43) Top 42" x 20". Height 17". ($550-650)

C 3549 G – Lamp Table (1939-42) Round top 22" in diameter. Height 26". ($550-650)

C 3997 C – Arm Chair (1941-42) Seat 22" x 22". Height of back 24". Spring filled, reversible seat cushion. ($800-900)

C 3977 W – Desk-Chest-Bookcase (1941-42) This is bookcase shown in large view. A compact unit particularly suited to apartment use. Width 60". Depth 12". Height 44". ($2,250-2,500)

C 3995 C – Arm Chair (1941-42) This is the open frame chair with upholstered, capped arm in large view. Seat 23" x 21". Height of back 21". ($1,250-1,350)

C 3990 LR – Leg Rest (1941-42) Size of top 25" x 21". Height 15". Top is fitted with reversible, spring filled cushion. ($450-550)

C 3976 W – Desk-Chest-Bookcase (1941-42) This is the smaller sized bookcase shown in cut-in view. It is 48" wide, 12" deep, and 44" high. ($1,850-2,000)

C 3980-68 – Davenport (1941-44) Seat 68" x 21". Height of back 21". Reversible, spring filled seat cushions. ($2,500-3,000)

C 3980 C – Arm Chair (1944) Seat 23" x 21". Height of back 21". Reversible, spring filled seat cushion. ($1,200-1,300)

C 3962 G – End Table (1941-42) Oval top measures 28" x 15". Height 21". ($800-900)

C 3942 G – Cocktail Table (1941-44) Size of top 36" x 19". Height 16". ($450-550)

C 3348 X – Corner Cabinet (1940-43) This corner cabinet is equally adaptable to dining room and living room use. It measures 24" wide, 14 ½" deep, and 65" high. Lower, closed compartment is fitted with shelf. ($1,200-1,400)

C 3973 – 3-Drawer Bookcase-Chest (1941-42) This piece is often used with the sectional bookcase pieces shown in the next picture, although it makes an excellent commode or simple chest for the living room. Top measures 28" x 14". Height 32 ½". ($750-850)

C 3974 – Pier Cabinet (1941-42) Fitted with 4 drawers. Size of top 16" x 14". Height 32 ½". ($750-850)

C 3970 – Straight-Front Bookcase (1941-44) This is the open, straight-front bookcase, two of which are shown in this view. Fitted with adjustable shelves. Top 36" x 11". Height 32 ½". ($600-700)

C 3971 – Corner Bookcase (1941-44) This is the open front bookcase in corner of the grouping shown. Overall measurements are 28" x 28". Height 32 ½". ($750-850)

C 3767 C – Reading Chair (1940-42) Seat 22" x 22". Height of back 24". Reversible, spring filled seat cushion. ($1,150-1,250)

C 3994 C – Channel Back Arm Chair (1941-44) Spring filled seat measures 20" x 22". No-sag spring filled back is 19". Not available in leather or leathercloth. ($950-1,050)

C 3389 G – Console or Game Table (1939-42) Top of table folds and pivots. Size of top open 30" square; folded 30" x 15". Height 28". ($950-1,000)

C 3934 – Kneehole Desk (1941-42) A dual purpose piece which also serves as a vanity base. Finished on back as well as front. Size of top 44" x 18". Height 29". ($1,150-1,250)

C 3765 C – Arm Chair (1940-42) Seat 22" x 20". Height of back 16". ($750-900)

C 3957 G – Gate-Leg Table
(1941-42) Dual purpose table
for dining, living, and general
apartment use. Top measures
36" x 60" with both leaves
extended. As shown here, top
measures 36" x 14". ($800-
1,000)

C 3777 WX – Kneehole Desk
(1941-42) This desk is fitted
with only 3 drawers as the
bookcase end takes up right
hand drawer space. It is an
immensely practical piece
which adds color to any room
when bright jacketed books
are used in end shelves. Top
measures 42" x 20". Height
29". ($750-850)

C 3530 A – Side Chair (1939-
42) Seat measures 18" x 17".
Height of back 16". ($175-
250)

C 3997 C – Arm Chair (1941-
42) Seat 22" x 22". Height of
back 24". Spring filled,
reversible seat cushion. ($800-
900)

C 3992 C – Arm Chair
(1941-42) Seat 20" x 18
½". Height of back 18 ½".
Not available in leather or
imitation leather. ($1,000-
1,100)

C 3908 – Radio Table
(1941-42) This also serves
as a night stand in our 3900
bedroom series (Catalina).
Open compartment will
accommodate most makes
of midget radios. Top 14" x
13". Height 25". ($200-225)

C 3757 – Table Desk
(1940-42) Fitted with
drawer. Top 36" x 18".
Height 29". ($800-900)

**C 3991 C – Wood Frame
Arm Chair** (1941-44) Seat
20" x 18 ½". Height of back
18 ½". ($900-1,000)

1950s – The Modern Years

Upholstered Chairs

M 340 C – Arm Chair (1950-53) The seat of this occasional pull-up chair is 22" wide and 21" deep. The back is 17" high. ($750-850)

M 342 C – Man's Lounge Chair (1950) This large arm chair has a reversible seat cushion that measures 21" wide by 22" deep. The back is 24" high. ($550-600)

M 341 C – Wing Chair (1950) A tightly upholstered pull-up chair with an extra high 21" back. The seat is 22" wide and 20" deep. ($550-600)

M 343 C – Ladies' Lounge Chair (1950) This arm chair has a seat 21" wide by 21" deep. The height of the back is 19". ($1,150-1,250)

M 345 C – Tub Chair (1950-58) The circular seat of this arm chair measures 24" wide by 22" deep. The back is 18" high. ($750-900)

M 346 C – Barrel Wing Chair (1950) The cushion measures 24" wide and 21" deep. The back is 21" high. ($1,000-1,200)

M 347 C – Pull-up Wing Chair (1950) This arm chair has a seat that is 22" wide and 18 ½" deep. The back is 20" high. ($550-650)

M 348 C – Pull up Occasional Chair (1950) This arm chair seat measures 19" wide and 20" deep. The back is 15 ½" high. ($550-650)

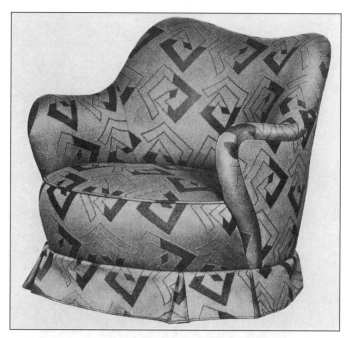

M 354 C – **Wheeled Television Chair** (1950-52) Fitted with ball bearing swivel wheels. Circular seat measures 24" wide by 22" deep. Height of back 18". Overall height 30". ($500-600)

M 564 C – **Swivel Tub Chair** (1951-52) Fitted with ball bearing Seng swivel mechanism. Width of seat 23". Depth of seat 19". Overall height 31 ½". ($650-750)

M 384 C – **Large Barrel Wing Chair** (1950-54) Reversible spring filled seat cushion measures 21" wide x 21" deep. Height of back 23". Overall height 38". ($1,250-1,450)

M 565 C – **High Back Easy Chair** (1951-52) Width of seat 23". Depth of seat 22". Overall height 35". ($900-1,000)

M 566 C – Barrel Wing Chair (1951-53) Width of seat 21". Depth of seat 21". Overall height 33". ($1,200-1,300)

M 568 C – Open Arm Tub Chair / Ladies' Club Chair (1951-58) Overall dimensions: 23" wide, 28" deep, 29 ½" high. ($900-1,000)

M 567 C – Ladies' Pull-up Chair (1951-53) Width of seat 21". Depth of seat 20". Overall height 32". ($900-1,000)

M 569 C – Pull-up Chair (1951-58) Overall dimensions: 28" wide, 27" deep, 32 ½" high. ($650-750)

M 558 C – Lounge Chair (1953-54) Width of seat 22". Depth of seat 20". Height of back 20". Overall height 34 ½". ($550-600)

M 85 C – Pull-up Chair (1952) Width of seat 22 ½". Depth 26". Height 32 ½". ($300-350)

M 598 C – Ladies' Club Chair (1953-54) Width of seat 19". Depth of seat 19". Height of back 16". Overall height 30". ($650-750)

M 559 C – High Back Lounge Chair (1952-58) Seat 22" wide x 20" deep. Back height 26". Overall dimensions: 28 ½" wide, 33" deep, 39 ½" high. ($650-750)

M 797 C – **High Back Barrel Chair** (1953-54) Width of seat 21 ½".
Depth of seat 21". Height of back 22". Overall height 34". ($800-900)

M 799 C – **Posture Back Arm Chair** (1953-54) Width of seat 22". Depth of seat 20 ½". Height of back 26". Overall height 37 ½". ($1,000-1,100)

M 941 C – **Arm Chair** (1954-55) Seat 23" wide x 19" deep. Back height 18". Overall dimensions: 30" wide, 28" deep, 31 ½" high. ($900-950)

M 798 C – **Open Arm Posture Back Arm Chair** (1953-54) Width of seat 22 ½". Depth of seat 20". Height of back 20". Overall height 32". ($800-900)

M 945 C – Club/Lounge Chair (1954-56) Seat 23" wide x 19" deep. Back height 18". Overall dimensions: 30" wide x 30" deep, 32 ½" high. ($800-900)

M 947 C – Lounge Chair (1954-56) Seat 22" wide x 20" deep. Back height 21". Overall dimensions: 30" wide, 35" deep, 34" high. ($800-900)

M 946 C – Ladies' Chair (1954-55) Seat 21" wide x 20" deep. Back height 18". Overall dimensions: 27" wide, 31" deep, 31 ½" high. ($800-900)

M 948 – Armless Pull-Up Chair (1954-56) Seat 23" wide x 21" deep. Back height 16". Overall dimensions: 23" wide, 25" deep, 32" high. ($250-300)

M 984 C – Wing Chair (1954-58) Seat 24" wide x 20" deep. Back height 20". Overall dimensions: 33" wide, 32" deep, 36" high. ($800-900)

M 1156 C – Wood Arm Pull-Up Chair (1955-56) Seat 22" wide x 18" deep. Back height 17 ½". Overall dimensions: 27" wide, 26" deep, 33" high. ($300-400)

M 1157 C – Pull-Up Chair (1955-58) Seat 20" wide x 22" deep. Back height 16 ½". Overall dimensions: 28" wide, 28" deep, 30" high. ($500-600)

M 1158 C – Danish Occasional Chair (1955-58) Seat 24" wide x 18" deep. Back height 16". Overall dimensions: 31" wide, 29" deep, 27 ½" high. ($1,050-1,150)

M 1159 C – High Back Barrel Chair (1955-56) Seat 25" wide x 20" deep. Back height 22". Overall dimensions: 32" wide, 31" deep, 33" high. ($650-750)

M 1163 C – Large Club Chair (1955-56) Fitted with 4 ball-bearing caster wheels. Seat 25" wide x 22" deep. Back height 17". Overall dimensions: 36" wide, 36" deep, 31" high. ($650-750)

M 1161 C – Ladies' Lounge Chair (1955-58) Seat 23" wide x 19" deep. Back height 15". Overall dimensions: 30" wide, 28" deep, 28" high. ($550-650)

M 1794 C – Ladies' Chair (1958) Overall dimensions: 31" wide, 32" deep, 27" high. ($300-400)

M 1796 C – Pillow-Back Arm Chair (1958) Overall dimensions: 30" wide, 34" deep, 35" high. ($300-400)

53

Sectionals, Davenports, and Love Seats

M 350 – Single Filler (1950); **M 350 LC or RC – Left or Right Arm Chair** (1950) The all-upholstered M 350 suite consists of the right arm chair (M 350 RC), straight single filler (M 350), and left arm unit (M 350 LC). The sizes of these pieces are identical to the similar pieces of the M 330 suite (see pages 55-57). ($300-350, $375-475)

M 352-68 – Davenport (1950) A large, roomy sofa that features smart design and comfort attributes. Between the arms, this davenport is 68" wide. The cushions are 22" deep and the back is 21" high. ($1,250-1,500)

M 316 G – Cocktail Table (1950) Fitted with a full length shelf, this table has a top that measures 36" x 19". It is 16" high. ($500-550)

M 350 C – Arm Chair (1950) Cushion is 23" wide and 22" deep. The back is 21" high. ($1,000-1,100)

M 317 G – End Table (1950) Matches the coffee table in the picture to the right. This convenient chairside piece, with its full length shelf, has a top 28" long by 14" wide. It stands arm height of 21". ($450-500)

M 353 – Curved Filler (1950) This picture emphasizes the fact that it is possible to create anything from a tête-à-tête grouping to a 100-foot cocktail lounge with sectional units. The M 333 and M 353 pieces are used in this unusual arrangement. ($650-750)

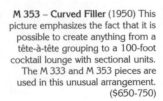

M 330 – Single Filler (1950) Width of cushion 23". Depth of cushion 22". Height of back 21". Overall height 32". ($500-550)

M 333 – Curved Single Filler (1950) Cushion width at front 22", at back 33". Depth of cushion 22". Height of back 21". Overall height 32". ($650-750)

M 330 C – Arm Chair (1950) Width of seat cushion 23". Depth of cushion 22". Height of back 21". Overall height 32". ($1,500-1,600)

M 331 – Double Filler (1950) Width of seat 48". Depth of seat 22". Height of back 21". Overall height 32". ($1,000-1,200)

M 331 LC or RC – Double Filler with Left or Right Arms (1950) Width of seat 48". Depth of seat 22". Height of back 21". Overall height 32". ($1,000-1,100)

M 330 LC or RC – Left or Right Arm Chair (1950) Width of cushion 23". Depth of cushion 22". Height of back 21". Overall height 32". ($750-850)

M 332-68 – Davenport (1950) Width between arms 68". Depth of cushions 22". Height of back 21". Overall height 32". ($2,250-2,500)

M 331-48 – Love Seat (1950) Width between arms 48". Depth of seat 22". Height of back 21". Overall height 32". ($1,750-2,000)

M 355 – Single Filler (1950-53) Width of cushion 23". Depth of cushion 22". Height of back 21". Overall height 32". ($400-500)

M 356 – Double Filler (1950-53) Width of seat 48". Depth of seat 22". Height of back 21". Overall height 32". ($750-850)

M 357 – Curved Single Filler (1950-52) Cushion width at front 22", at back 33". Depth of cushion 22". Height of back 21". Overall height 32". ($650-750)

M 356 LC or RC – Double Filler with Left or Right Arms (1950-53) Width of seat 48". Depth of seat 22". Height of back 21". Overall height 32". ($750-850)

M 355 LC or RC – Left or Right Arm Chair (1950-53) Width of cushion 23". Depth of cushion 22". Height of back 21". Overall height 32". ($550-650)

M 355 C – Arm Chair (1950-53) Width of seat cushion 23". Depth of cushion 22". Height of back 21". Overall height 32". ($1,050-1,200)

M 358-68 – **Davenport** (1950-53) Width between arms 68". Depth of cushions 22". Height of back 21". Overall height 32". ($1,750-2,000)

M 356-48 – **Love Seat** (1950-53) Width between arms 48". Depth of seat 22". Height of back 21". Overall height 32". ($1,750-2,000)

M 560 – **Single Filler** (1951-53) Width of cushion 23". Depth of cushion 22". Height of back 21". Overall height 32". ($500-550)

M 563 – Curved Single Filler (1951-52)
Cushion width at front 22", at back 33". Depth
of cushion 22". Height of back 21". Overall
height 32". ($550-600)

M 561 – Double Filler (1951-53) Width of seat 48".
Depth of seat 22". Height of back 21". Overall height 32".
($650-750)

M 560 LC or RC – Left or Right Arm Chair (1951-53) Width of cushion 23".
Depth of cushion 22". Height of back 21". Overall height 32". ($750-900)

M 561 LC or RC – Double Filler with Right or Left Arm (1951-53) Width of seat 48". Depth of seat 22". Height of back 21". Overall height 32". ($1,000-1,200)

M 560 C – Arm Chair (1951-53) Width of seat cushion 23". Depth of cushion 22". Height of back 21". Overall height 32". ($1,250-1,350)

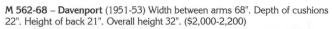

M 561-48 – Love Seat (1951-53) Width between arms 48". Depth of seat 22". Height of back 21". Overall height 32". ($1,700-1,800)

M 562-68 – Davenport (1951-53) Width between arms 68". Depth of cushions 22". Height of back 21". Overall height 32". ($2,000-2,200)

M 595 RC or LC – Right or Left Arm Chair (1952-55) Width of seat 26". Depth of seat 22". Overall height 30". ($550-600)

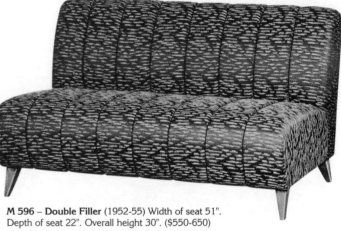

M 596 – Double Filler (1952-55) Width of seat 51". Depth of seat 22". Overall height 30". ($550-650)

M 596 LC or RC – Double Filler with Right or Left Arm (1952-55) Width of seat 51". Depth of seat 22". Overall height 30". ($650-750)

M 595 – Single Filler (1952-55) Width of seat 26". Depth of seat 22". Overall height 30". ($375-475)

The pieces in this next grouping (shown below and on page 64) were advertised as "Exclusive West Coast Patterns."

M 595 C – Arm Chair (1952-55) Width of seat 26".
Depth of seat 22". Overall height 30". ($1,150-1,250)

M 596-51 – Love Seat (1952-55) Width of seat 51".
Depth of seat 22". Overall height 30". ($1,550-1,850)

M 5608-28 – Single Filler (1952) Width of seat 28".
Depth of seat 22 ½". Height of back 15". Overall
height 32 ½". Overall depth 36 ½". ($200-300)
M 5608 LR – Leg Rest (1952) Top measures 28"
square. Height 17". ($650-750)

M 597-76 – Davenport (1952-55) Width of seat 76".
Depth of seat 22". Overall height 30". ($2,500-2,700)

M 5608 L & R – Left and Right Arm Sectional (1952) Overall length of each piece 40". Overall depth 36 ½". Overall height 32 ½". Depth of seat 22 ½". Height of back 15". ($650-750)

M 5608 C – Club Chair (1952) This club chair is 36" wide and 37" deep. Height 32". ($400-500)

M 5608-95 – Armless Davenport (1952) Overall length 95". Overall depth 36 ½". Overall height 32 ½". Depth of seat 22 ½". Height of back 15". ($1,550-1,800)

M 5628-78 – Davenport (1952) Overall length 78". Depth of seat 21". Height of back 16". Overall height 31". ($2,750-3,000)

M 5608-100 – Davenport (1952) Overall length 100". Overall depth 36 ½". Overall height 32 ½". Depth of seat 22 ½". Height of back 15". ($1,550-1,800)

These pieces were the same as the M 355 grouping from a few years earlier (see pages 57-59), but with different style numbers.

M 956 – **Double Filler** (1953-54) Width of seat 48". Depth of seat 22". Height of back 21". Overall height 32". ($500-600)

M 955 – **Single Filler** (1953-54) Width of cushion 23". Depth of cushion 22". Height of back 21". Overall height 32". ($400-500)

M 956 LC or RC – **Double Filler with Left or Right Arm** (1953-54) Width of seat 48". Depth of seat 22". Height of back 21". Overall height 32". ($600-700)

M 955 LC or RC – **Left or Right Arm Chair** (1953-54) Width of cushion 23". Depth of cushion 22". Height of back 21". Overall height 32". ($500-600)

M 955 C – **Arm Chair** (1953-54) Width of seat cushion 23". Depth of cushion 22". Height of back 21". Overall height 32". ($1,050-1,150)

M 956-48 – **Love Seat** (1953-54) Width between arms 48".
Depth of seat 22". Height of back 21". Overall height 32".
($1,500-1,650)

M 958-68 – **Davenport** (1953-54) Width between arms 68".
Depth of cushions 22". Height of back 21". Overall height 32".
($1,750-2,000)

These pieces were the same as the M 560 grouping from a few years earlier (see pages 59-61), but with different style numbers.

M 960 – **Single Filler** (1953-54) Width of cushion 23". Depth of cushion 22". Height of back 21". Overall height 32". ($400-500)

M 960 LC or RC – **Left or Right Arm Chair** (1953-54) Width of cushion 23".
Depth of cushion 22". Height of back 21". Overall height 32". ($750-850)

M 961 – **Double Filler** (1953-54) Width of seat 48".
Depth of seat 22". Height of back 21". Overall height 32".
($500-600)

M 961 LC or RC – Double Filler with Left or Right Arm (1953-54) Width of seat 48". Depth of seat 22". Height of back 21". Overall height 32". ($900-1,000)

M 961-48 – Love Seat (1953-54) Width between arms 48". Depth of seat 22". Height of back 21". Overall height 32". ($1,600-1,800)

M 965 – Single Filler (1953-54) Width of cushion 23". Depth of cushion 22". Height of back 22". Overall height 32". ($400-500)

M 965 LC or RC – Left or Right Arm Chair (1953-54) Width of cushion 23". Depth of cushion 22". Height of back 22". Overall height 32". ($550-650)

M 965 C – Arm Chair (1953-54) Width of seat cushion 23". Depth of cushion 22". Height of back 22". Overall height 32". ($1,050-1,150)

M 966 – Double Filler (1953-54) Width of seat 48". Depth of seat 22". Height of back 22". Overall height 32". ($500-600)

M 966-48 – Love Seat (1953-54) Width between arms 48". Depth of seat 22". Height of back 22". Overall height 32". ($1,550-1,650)

M 966 LC or RC – Double Filler with Left or Right Arm (1953-54) Width of seat 48". Depth of seat 22". Height of back 22". Overall height 32". ($750-850)

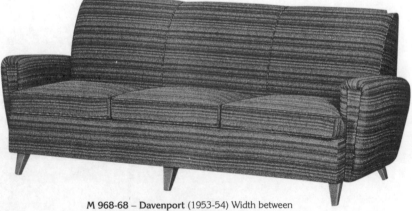

M 968-68 – Davenport (1953-54) Width between arms 68". Depth of cushion 22". Height of back 22". Overall height 32". ($1,750-2,000)

M 755 – Single Filler (1954-55) Seat, 24" wide x 21" deep. Back height 15".
Overall dimensions: 24" wide, 33" deep, 29 ½" high. ($300-400)

M 755 LC or RC – Left or Right Arm Chair (1954-55) Seat, 24" wide x 21"
deep. Back height 15". Overall dimensions: 29" wide, 33" deep, 29 ½" high.
($450-550)

M 756 – Double Filler (1954-55) Seat, 48" wide x 21" deep. Back height 15". Overall dimensions: 48" wide, 33" deep, 29 ½" high. ($400-500)

M 756 LC or RC – Double Filler with Right or Left Arm (1954-55) Seat, 48" wide x 21" deep. Back height 15". Overall dimensions: 53" wide, 33" deep, 29 ½" high. ($650-750)

M 756-48 – Love Seat (1954-55) Seat, 48" wide x 21" deep. Back height 15". Overall dimensions: 58" wide, 33" deep, 29 ½" high. ($1,200-1,300)

M 758-68 – Davenport (1954-55) Seat, 68" wide x 21" deep. Back height 15". Overall dimensions: 78" wide, 33" deep, 29 ½" high. ($1,550-1,800)

M 755 C – Arm Chair (1954-55) Seat, 24" wide x 21" deep. Back height 15". Overall dimensions: 34" wide, 33" deep, 29 ½" high. ($900-1,000)

M 935 – Single Filler (1954-56) Seat, 24" wide x 21" deep. Back height 16". Overall dimensions: 24" wide, 34" deep, 31" high. ($300-400)

M 935 LC or RC – Left or Right Arm Chair (1954-56) Seat, 24" wide x 21" deep. Back height 16". Overall dimensions: 28" wide, 34" deep, 31" high. ($500-600)

M 936 – Double Filler (1954-56) Seat, 48" wide x 21" deep. Back height 16". Overall dimensions: 48" wide, 34" deep, 31" high. ($600-700)

M 936 LC or RC – Double Filler with Right or Left Arm (1954-56) Seat, 48" wide x 21" deep. Back height 16". Overall dimensions: 52" wide, 34" deep, 31" high. ($650-750)

M 936-48 – Love Seat (1954-56) Seat, 48" wide x 21" deep. Back height 16". Overall dimensions: 56" wide, 34" deep, 31" high. ($1,200-1,300)

M 937-84 – Davenport Sleeper (1954-56) The reversible, foam rubber mattress measures 75" x 30". Seat, 75" wide x 21" deep. Back height 16". Overall dimensions: 84" wide, 34" deep, 31" high. ($1,550-1,650)

M 935 C – Arm Chair (1954-56) Seat, 24" wide x 21" deep. Back height 16". Overall dimensions: 32" wide, 34" deep, 31" high. ($1,000-1,100)

M 975 – Single Filler (1954-58) Seat, 24" wide x 21" deep. Back height 16". Overall dimensions: 24" wide, 33" deep, 29 ½" high. ($300-400)

M 975 LC or RC – Left or Right Arm Chair (1954-58) Seat, 24" wide x 21" deep. Back height 16". Overall dimensions: 29" wide, 33" deep, 29 ½" high. ($500-600)

M 975 C – **Arm Chair** (1954-58) Seat, 24" wide x 21" deep. Back height 16". Overall dimensions: 34" wide, 33" deep, 29 ½" high. ($900-1,000)

M 986 – **Double Filler** (1954-58) Seat, 48" wide x 21" deep. Back height 16". Overall dimensions: 48" wide, 33" deep, 29 ½" high. ($600-700)

M 986-48 – **Love Seat** (1954-58) Seat, 48" wide x 21" deep. Back height 16". Overall dimensions: 58" wide, 33" deep, 29 ½" high. ($1,200-1,300)

M 986 LC or RC – **Double Filler with Left or Right Arm** (1954-58) Seat, 48" wide x 21" deep. Back height 16". Overall dimensions: 53" wide, 33" deep, 29 ½" high. ($650-750)

M 988-68 – **Davenport** (1954-58) Seat, 68" wide x 21" deep. Back height 16". Overall dimensions: 78" wide, 33" deep, 29 ½" high. ($1,550-1,800)

M 980 – Single Filler (1954-55) Seat, 24" wide x 21" deep. Back height 15". Overall dimensions: 24" wide, 33" deep, 29 ½" high. ($300-400)

M 980 LC or RC – Left or Right Arm Chair (1954-55) Seat, 24" wide x 21" deep. Back height 15". Overall dimensions: 28" wide, 33" deep, 29 ½" high. ($500-600)

M 981 – Double Filler (1954-55) Seat, 48" wide x 21" deep. Back height 15". Overall dimensions: 48" wide, 33" deep, 29 ½" high. ($600-700)

M 981-48 – Love Seat (1954-55) Seat, 48" wide x 21" deep. Back height 15". Overall dimensions: 56" wide, 33" deep, 29 ½" high. ($700-800)

M 981 LC or RC – Double Filler with Left or Right Arm (1954-55) Seat, 48" wide x 21" deep. Back height 15". Overall dimensions: 52" wide, 33" deep, 29 ½" high. ($650-750)

M 982-68 – Davenport (1954-55) Seat, 68" wide x 21" deep. Back height 15". Overall dimensions: 76" wide, 33" deep, 29 ½" high. ($1,500-1,800)

M 980 C – Arm Chair (1954-55) Seat, 24" wide x 21" deep. Back height 15". Overall dimensions: 32" wide, 33" deep, 29 ½" high. ($600-700)

These specialty filler units were designed to increase the flexibility of the various sectional groupings and allow for some especially dramatic arrangements.

M 977 L or M 977 R – Left and Right Bumper End-offs (1954-58) The right hand side sitting (R) is shown at top. The left hand side sitting (L) is shown below. Seat, 61" wide x 21" deep. Back height 15". Overall dimensions: 61" wide, 33" deep, 29 ½" high. ($800-1,000)

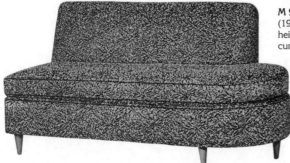

M 979 L or M 979 R – Left and Right Asymmetrical Curved Units (1954-55) Seat, 42" at front, 60" at back. Depth of seat 21". Back height 15". Overall dimensions: 66" wide, 33" on straight side, 38" at curve, 29 ½" high. ($650-750)

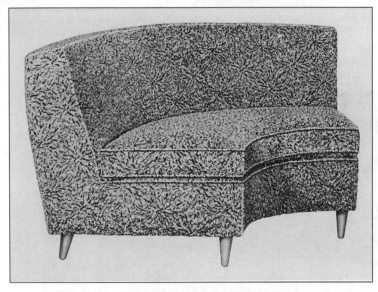

M 987 – **Quarter-Round Filler** (1954-58) Seat, 28 ½" at front, 60" at back. Depth of seat 21". Back height 15". Overall dimensions: 72" wide, 33" deep, 29 ½" high. ($550-650)

M 1167 LC or RC – **Left or Right Arm Double Filler** (1955-58) Seat, 52" wide x 21" deep. Back height 18". Overall dimensions: 57" wide, 32" deep, 31" high. ($750-850)

M 1167-52 – **Love Seat** (1955-58) Seat, 52" wide x 21" deep. Back height 18". Overall dimensions: 58" wide, 62" deep, 31" high. ($1,000-1,200)

M 1167 – **Double Filler** (1955-58) Seat, 52" wide x 21" deep. Back height 18". Overall dimensions: 52" wide, 32" deep, 31" high. ($700-800)

M 1168 – Armless Davenport (1955-58) Seat, 84" wide x 21" deep. Back height 18". Overall dimensions: 84" wide, 32" deep, 31" high. ($1,500-1,800)

M 1168-84 – Davenport (1955-58) Seat, 84" wide x 21" deep. Back height 18". Overall dimensions: 94" wide, 32" deep, 31" high. ($1,800-2,200)

M 1170 – Single Filler (1955-58) Seat, 25" wide x 21" deep. Back height 17". Overall dimensions: 25" wide, 33" deep, 29" high. ($600-700)

M 1170 LC or RC – Left or Right Arm Chair (1955-58) Seat, 25" wide x 21" deep. Back height 17". Overall dimensions: 29" wide, 33" deep, 29" high. ($600-700)

M 1170 C – Arm Chair (1955-58) Seat, 25" wide x 21" deep. Back height 17". Overall dimensions: 33" wide, 33" deep, 29" high. ($650-750)

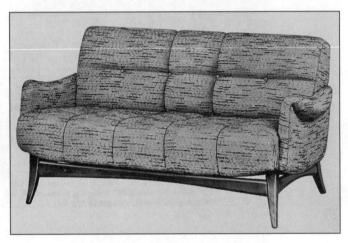

M 1171-50 – Love Seat (1955-58) Seat, 50" wide x 21" deep. Back height 17". Overall dimensions: 58" wide, 33" deep, 29" high. ($1,000-1,200)

M 1171 – Double Filler (1955-58) Seat, 50" wide x 21" deep. Back height 17". Overall dimensions: 50" wide, 33" deep, 29" high. ($800-1,000)

M 1171 LC or RC – Right or Left Arm Double Filler (1955-58) Seat, 50" wide x 21" deep. Back height 17". Overall dimensions: 54" wide, 33" deep, 29" high. ($650-750)

M 1172-75 – **Davenport** (1955-58) Seat, 75" wide x 21" deep. Back height 17".
Overall dimensions: 83" wide, 33" deep, 29" high. ($2,200-2,500)

M 1195 LC or RC – **Left or Right Arm Chair** (1955-56) Seat, 26" wide x 22"
deep. Back height 17". Overall dimensions: 30" wide, 35" deep, 30" high.
($500-600)

M 1196 – **Double Filler** (1955-56) Seat, 51" wide x 22" deep. Back height 17".
Overall dimensions: 51" wide, 35" deep, 30" high. ($700-800)

M 1195 – **Single Filler** (1955-56) Seat, 26" wide x 22" deep. Back height 17".
Overall dimensions: 26" wide, 35" deep, 30" high. ($400-500)

M 1197-76 – Davenport (1955-56) Seat, 76" wide x 22" deep. Back height 17". Overall dimensions: 84" wide, 35" deep, 30" high. ($2,250-2,500)

The pieces shown below and on page 83 were advertised in the 1958 catalog as "The 'Monterey' Group."

M 1196 LC or RC – Left or Right Arm Double Filler (1955-56) Seat, 51" wide x 22" deep. Back height 17". Overall dimensions: 55" wide, 35" deep, 30" high. ($650-850)

M 1195 C – Arm Chair (1955-56) Seat, 26" wide x 22" deep. Back height 17". Overall dimensions: 34" wide, 35" deep, 30" high. ($1,000-1,100)

M 1196-51 – Love Seat (1955-56) Seat, 51" wide x 22" deep. Back height 17". Overall dimensions: 59" wide, 35" deep, 30" high. ($1,250-1,500)

M 1785 – Single Filler (Monterey) (1958) Overall dimensions: 24" wide, 34" deep, 29" high. ($200-300)

M 1785 RC or LC – Right or Left Arm Chair (Monterey) (1958) Overall
dimensions: 28" wide, 34" deep, 29" high. ($400-500)

M 1785 C – Arm Chair (Monterey) (1958) Overall
dimensions: 32" wide, 34" deep, 29" high. ($400-500)

M 1786 – Double Filler (Monterey) (1958) Overall
dimensions: 48" wide, 34" deep, 29" high. ($400-500)

M 1786-56 – Love Seat (Monterey) (1958) Overall
dimensions: 56" wide, 34" deep, 29" high. ($500-700)

**M 1786 RC or LC – Right or Left Arm Sofa
(Monterey)** (1958) Overall dimensions: 52" wide,
34" deep, 29" high. ($500-700)

M 1787-80 – Sofa (Monterey) (1958) Overall dimensions: 80" wide, 34" deep,
29" high. ($1,000-1,500)

These pieces were advertised in the 1958 catalog as "The 'Gramercy Park' Group."

M 1790 RC or LC – **Right or Left Arm Chair (Gramercy Park)** (1958) Overall dimensions: 30" wide, 34" deep, 29" high. ($300-400)

M 1791 – **Double Filler (Gramercy Park)** (1958) Overall dimensions: 48" wide, 34" deep, 29" high. ($400-500)

M 1790 – **Single Filler (Gramercy Park)** (1958) Overall dimensions: 24" wide, 34" deep, 29" high. ($200-300)

M 1791 RC or LC – **Right or Left Arm Sofa (Gramercy Park)** (1958) Overall dimensions: 54" wide, 34" deep, 29" high. ($500-600)

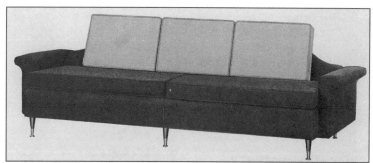

M 1793-96 – Pillow-Back Sofa (Gramercy Park) (1958) Overall dimensions: 96" wide, 34" deep, 30" high. ($900-1,200)

M 1790 C – Arm Chair (Gramercy Park) (1958) Overall dimensions: 36" wide, 34" deep, 29" high. ($500-600)

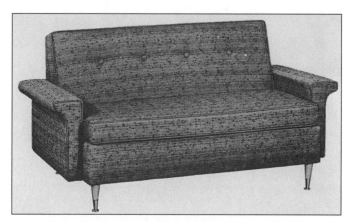

M 1791-60 – Love Seat (Gramercy Park) (1958) Overall dimensions: 60" wide, 34" deep, 29" high. ($600-700)

M 1788 – Quarter Round (Monterey/Gramercy Park) (1958) Overall dimensions: 72" wide, 34" deep, 29" high. ($350-450)

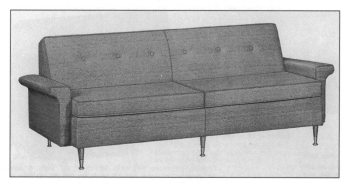

M 1792-84 – Sofa (Gramercy Park) (1958) Overall dimensions: 84" wide, 34" deep, 29" high. ($800-1,000)

M 1789 R or L – Right or Left Bumper End-off (Monterey/Gramercy Park) (1958) Overall dimensions: 48" wide, 34" deep, 29" high. ($500-600)

Aristocraft Line

The Aristocraft line consisted of three styles of loose cushion upholstered pieces (rounded cushions, box and welted cushions, and balloon cushions) all with a decidedly informal, comfortable appearance, as well as a group of occasional tables. Aristocraft upholstered pieces are shown separately here, but the occasional tables have been incorporated with all other occasional tables in the section immediately following this one (pages 94-109). In their catalogs, Heywood-Wakefield advised that although the Aristocraft tables were designed to be used with Aristocraft upholstered pieces, they were in fact "widely displayed and sold with other H-W Modern suites, sectionals, and occasional chairs." All Aristocraft pieces can be identified by a "CM" prefix in the model numbers.

CM 367 – **Single Filler** (1950-54) Width of seat 22". Depth of seat 21". Height of back 19". Overall height 32". ($400-500)

CM 367 LC or RC – **Left or Right Arm Chair** (1950-54) Width of seat 22". Depth of seat 21". Height of back 19". Overall height 32". ($500-600)

CM 367 C – Arm Chair (1950-54) Width of seat 22". Depth of seat 21". Height of back 19". Overall height 32". ($1,050-1,150)

CM 368 LC or RC – Double Filler with Left or Right Arms (1950-54) Width of seat 44". Depth of seat 21". Height of back 19". Overall height 32". ($750-850)

CM 368 – Double Filler (1950-54) Width of seat 44". Depth of seat 21". Height of back 19". Overall height 32". ($750-850)

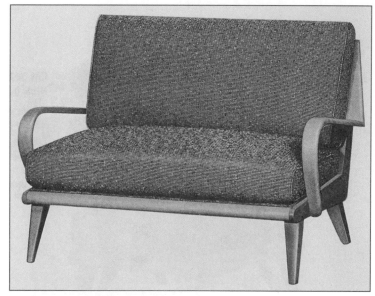

CM 368-44 – Love Seat (1950-54) Width of seat 44". Depth of seat 21". Height of back 19". Overall height 32". ($1,150-1,350)

CM 369-66 – **Davenport** (1950-54) Width of seat 66". Depth of seat 21". Height of back 19". Overall height 32". ($1,550-1,800)

CM 388 C – **Arm Chair** (1950-54) Width of seat 23". Depth of seat 22". Height of back 23". Overall height 35". ($800-900)

CM 388 – **Single Filler** (1950-54)
Width of seat 23". Depth of seat 22".
Height of back 23". Overall height 35".
($500-600)

CM 388 LC or RC – **Left or Right Arm Chair**
(1950-54) Width of seat 23". Depth of seat 22".
Height of back 23". Overall height 35". ($600-700)

CM 367 D – **Platform Rocker** (1952-54) Width of seat 22". Depth of seat 21". Height of back 25". Overall height 37". ($900-1,000)

CM 367 R – **High Back Arm Chair** (1952-54) Width of seat 22". Depth of seat 21". Height of back 25". Overall height 39". ($1,150-1,250)

CM 727 LC or RC – **Left or Right Arm Chair** (1952-54) Width of seat 22". Depth of seat 21". Height of back 19". Overall height 32". ($500-600)

CM 727 – **Single Filler** (1952-54) Width of seat 22". Depth of seat 21". Height of back 19". Overall height 32". ($350-450)

CM 727 C – **Arm Chair** (1952-54) Width of seat 22". Depth of seat 21". Height of back 19". Overall height 32". ($1,050-1,150)

CM 727 D – **Platform Rocker** (1952-54) Width of seat 22".
Depth of seat 21". Height of back 25". Overall height 37".
($1,250-1,350)

CM 727 R – **High Back Arm Chair**
(1952-54) Width of seat 22". Depth
of seat 21". Height of back 25".
Overall height 39". ($1,150-1,250)

CM 728 – **Double Filler** (1952-54) Width of seat 44".
Depth of seat 21". Height of back 19". ($550-650)

CM 728 LC or RC – **Double Filler with Right or Left Arm** (1952-54) Width of
seat 44". Depth of seat 21". Height of back 19". Overall height 32". ($750-850)

CM 728-44 – **Love Seat** (1952-54) Width of seat 44". Depth of seat 21". Height
of back 19". Overall height 32". ($1,150-1,250)

90

CM 729-66 – **Davenport** (1952-54) Width of seat 66".
Depth of seat 21". Height of back 19". ($1,550-1,800)

CM 724 C – **Lounge Chair with Rubber Seat and Back Cushions** (1953-54)
Width of seat 22". Depth of seat 21". Height of back 19". Overall height 32".
($800-900)

CM 927 LC or RC – **Left or Right Arm Chair** (1954-58) Seat 22" wide x 21"
deep. Back height 19". Overall dimensions: 25" wide, 34" deep, 31" high.
($400-500)

CM 927 C – **Arm Chair** (1954-63) Seat 22" wide x 21" deep.
Back height 19". Overall dimensions: 28" wide, 34" deep, 31"
high. ($800-900)

**CM 927 – Single
Filler** (1954-58)
Seat 22" wide x 21"
deep. Back height
19". Overall
dimensions: 22"
wide, 34" deep, 31"
high. ($300-400)

CM 931 – **Double Filler** (1954-58) Seat 44" wide x 21" deep. Back height 19". Overall dimensions: 44" wide, 34" deep, 31" high. ($500-600)

CM 932-66 – **Davenport** (1954-58) Seat 66" wide x 21" deep. Back height 19". Overall dimensions: 72" wide, 34" deep, 31" high. ($1,250-1,450)

CM 931 LC or RC – **Double Filler with Right or Left Arm** (1954-58) Seat 44" wide x 21" deep. Back height 19". Overall dimensions: 47" wide, 34" deep, 31" high. ($600-700)

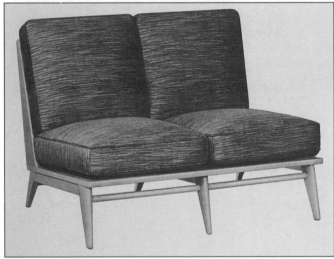

CM 928 – **Double Filler** (1954) Width of seat 44". Depth of seat 21". Overall width 44". Overall depth 34". Overall height 31". ($400-500)

CM 931-44 – **Love Seat** (1954-58) Seat 44" wide x 21" deep. Back height 19". Overall dimensions: 50" wide, 34" deep, 31" high. ($1,000-1,100)

CM 928 LC or RC – Double Filler with Left or Right Arm (1954) Width of seat 44". Depth of seat 21". Overall width 47". Overall depth 34". Overall height 31". ($600-700)

CM 931-50 – Love Seat (1958) Overall dimensions: 50" wide, 34" deep, 31" high. ($1,000-1,100)

CM 928-44 – Love Seat (1954) Width of seat 44". Depth of seat 21". Overall width 50". Overall depth 34". Overall height 31". ($1,000-1,100)

CM 932-72 – Davenport (1958-63) Overall dimensions: 72" wide, 34" deep, 31" high. ($1,250-1,450)

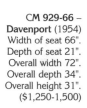

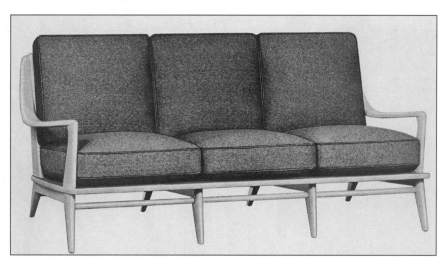

CM 929-66 – Davenport (1954) Width of seat 66". Depth of seat 21". Overall width 72". Overall depth 34". Overall height 31". ($1,250-1,500)

Occasional Tables

M 318 G – Lamp Table (1950) Top measures 21" x 21". Height 21". ($500-550)

Lamp Tables

M 337 G – **Lamp Table** (1950-53) Top measures 21" x 21". Shelf is 19" x 19". Height 25". ($350-450)

M 364 G – **Lamp Table** (1950-55) Size of top 26" x 24". Height 26". Size of shelf 21" x 21". ($450-550)

CM 373 G – **Lamp Table** (Aristocraft, 1950-52) The moulded and shaped top of this table is 20" x 18". Height 25". Useful as a night stand, too. The shelf is full length. ($300-400)

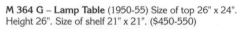

M 502 G – Lamp Table (1952) Top measures 21" x 21". Height 25". ($450-550)

M 993 G – Lamp Table with Shelf (1954-55) Top measures 22" x 20". Height 25". ($500-550)

CM 973 G – Lamp Table with Shelf (Aristocraft, 1954-55) Top measures 20" x 18". Height 25". ($300-400)

M 793 G – Lamp Table with Drawer (1953-55) Fitted with full length drawer. Top measures 20" x 18". Height 25". ($550-700)

M 1153 G – Lamp/Night Table (1955-59) Fitted with drawer and shelf. Top measures 24" x 24". Height 22". ($250-300)

M 1573 G – Lamp Table (1956) Top measures 22" x 22". Height 22". Also available with plastic top—order as M 1573 GP. ($450-550)

M 1503 G – Lamp Table with Shelf (1957-62) Top measures 26" wide by 24" deep. The shelf is 22 ½" wide by 20 ½" deep. Shelf height is 15". Overall height 21". ($375-475)

M 1583 G – Lamp Table (1956-58) Fitted with drawer and shelf. Top measures 26" x 24". Height 24". ($500-600)

CM 1703 G – Lamp Table (Aristocraft, 1958) Top is 20" x 18". Shelf measures 19 ½" x 17 ½". Overall height 21". ($250-350)

M 1586 G – Lamp Table (1956-58) Top measures 26" x 24". Height 26". ($450-550)

M 1588 G – Lamp Table (1958-60) Top measures 26" x 24". Height 26". ($300-400)

Cocktail Tables

Note: The M 316 G Cocktail Table is shown on page 54.

M 335 G – Cocktail Table (1950-54) Size of top 36" x 19". Size of shelf 31 ¾" x 16 ¾". Height 16". ($500-600)

M 306 G – Round Cocktail Table (1950-55) The round, revolving top measures 32" in diameter. Height 16". ($500-600)

M 307 G – Square Cocktail Table (1950-52) Top measures 36" square. Height 16". ($550-650)

M 392 G – Square Cocktail Table (1950-55) This table is also useful as a low corner table. Size of slightly off-square top 36" x 36". Height 16". ($750-950)

M 319 G – Cocktail Table (1950-55) The moulded and tapered top of this table measures 40" x 22". Height 16". ($500-600)

CM 371 G – Cocktail Coffee Table (Aristocraft, 1950-54) The moulded, shaped top of this table is 36" x 19". Height 16". ($300-400)

M 500 G – Cocktail Table (1952-53) Size of top 40" x 19". Height 16". ($550-650)

M 6321 G – Cocktail Table (1952) Top measures 48" x 24". Height 16". ($400-500)

M 795 G – Large Cocktail Table (1953-55) This king-size cocktail table has a 50" x 22" top. Height 16". ($700-800)

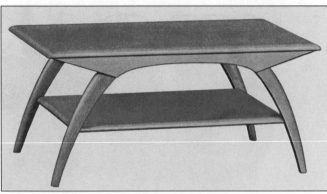

M 991 G – Cocktail Table with Shelf (1954-55) The top measures 36" x 19". Height 16". ($550-650)

M 905 G – Cocktail Table with Drawers (1955) Fitted with full length drawer. Top measures 40" x 20". Height 16". ($800-1,000)

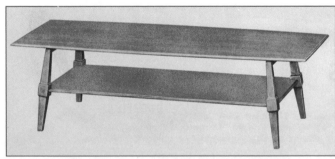

M 1151 G – Large Cocktail Table with Shelf (1955-59) Surfboard-shaped top measures 52" x 20". Height 16". ($200-300)

CM 971 G – Cocktail Table (Aristocraft, 1954-55) The moulded, shaped top of this table is 36" x 19". Height 16". ($200-300)

M 1155 G – Square Cocktail Table (1955-58) Fitted with four compartments and sliding door partitions on each side. Top measures 40" x 40". Height 15". ($350-450)

M 1576 G – Revolving Top Cocktail Table (1956-61) Revolving top measures 32" in diameter. Height 15". ($450-550)

M 1165 G – Oval Cocktail Table (1956-59) Top measures 40" x 30". Height 16". ($300-400)

M 1578 G – Round Cocktail Table (1956) Top measures 38" in diameter. Height 16". ($400-450)

M 1571 G – Cocktail Table (1956) Top measures 44" x 20". Height 14". This table is also available with plastic top—order as M 1571 GP. ($300-350)

M 1579 G – Square Cocktail Table (1956) Top measures 36" x 36". Height 16". ($400-450)

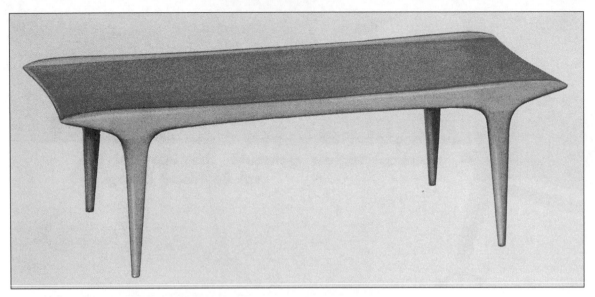

M 1580 G – Cocktail Table (1956-58) Top measures 50" x 22". Height 15". ($400-500)

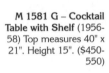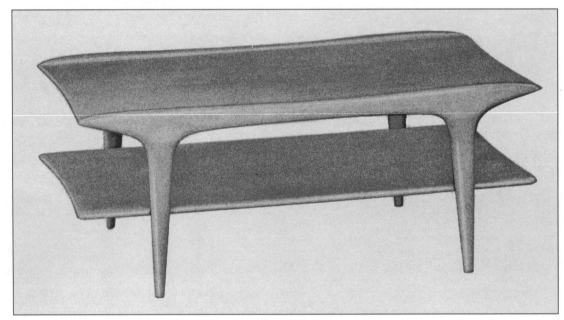

M 1581 G – Cocktail Table with Shelf (1956-58) Top measures 40" x 21". Height 15". ($450-550)

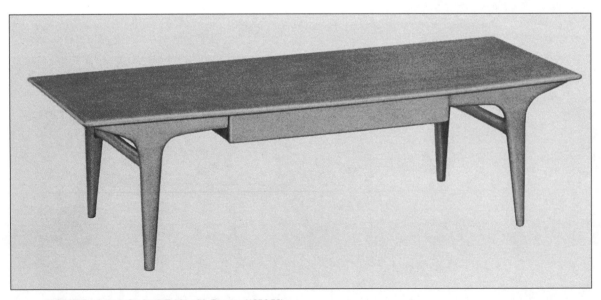

M 1585 G – Large Cocktail Table with Drawer (1956-58)
Top measures 54" x 22". Height 15". ($500-600)

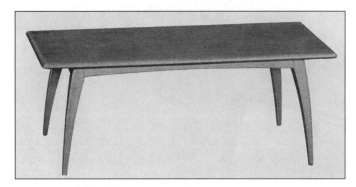

M 1501 G – Cocktail Table (1957-61) Top measures 42" long by 20" deep. Height 15". ($300-350)

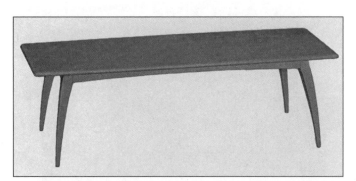

M 1505 G – Large Cocktail Table (1957-63) Top measures 52" long by 20" deep. Height 15". ($400-450)

M 1506 G – Cocktail/Corner Table (1957-58) Designed for use as square cocktail or low corner table. Top measures 32" square. Height 15". ($300-400)

M 1508 G – Round Cocktail Table (1957-63) Top measures 36" in diameter. Height 15". ($300-400)

CM 1701 G – Cocktail Table (Aristocraft, 1958) Top measures 36" x 19". Height is 15". ($350-450)

End Tables

Note: The M 317 G End Table is shown on page 54.

CM 372 G – **End Table** (Aristocraft, 1950-54) The moulded, shaped top is 28" long and 15" deep. The shelf is full length. Height 21". ($300-400)

M 391 G – **End Table** (1950-52) Top and shelf measure 28" x 16". Height 22". ($400-500)

M 501 G – **End Table** (1952-53) Size of top 28" x 16". Height 21". ($450-550)

M 395 – **Record Cabinet End Table** (1950-53) Aside from serving as a record cabinet or end table, this design offers general utility use. It is ideal height as a television table when used in conjunction with deep-cushioned upholstered units. Suitable for 12" record albums. Fitted with 3 compartments for useful storage. Size of top 28" x 16 ½". Height 22". ($1,150-1,350)

M 791 G – **End Table** (1952-54) Top measures 28" x 16". Height 21". ($450-550)

M 503 G – Magazine Rack End Table (1953-58)
Top measures 28" x 15". Height 22". ($500-600)

M 992 G – End Table with Shelf (1954-55) The top
measures 28" x 16". Height 21". ($450-550)

CM 972 G – End Table with Shelf (1954-55) The moulded, shaped top is 28"
long and 15" deep. The shelf is full length. Height 21". ($300-350)

M 1502 G – End Table with Shelf (1957-63) Top measures
30" long by 20" deep. The shelf is 26 ½" long by 16 ½"
deep. Shelf height 15". Overall height 21". ($300-350)

CM 1702 G – End Table (Aristocraft, 1958) Top measures 28" x
15". Shelf is 27 ½" x 14 ½". Overall height 21". ($250-300)

Step-End Tables

M 3753 G – Step-End Table (1952) Top measures 14 ½" x 16 ½". Middle and bottom shelf measure 30" x 15". Overall height 22". ($500-600)

M 308 G – Step-End Table (1950-54) This tier-topped table is 22" high. The cushion-height lower shelf measures 30" x 17". ($300-350)

M 794 G – Step-End Table with Drawer (1953-55) Fitted with full depth drawer. Cushion height shelf measures 30" x 18". Overall height 22". ($550-650)

M 906 G – Wedge Step-End Table (1954-55) Length of shelf 30". Width at back 22", at front 12". Height 22 ½". ($400-500)

CM 374 G – Step End Table (Aristocraft, 1950-53) The top of this tier table is 22" x 15". Overall height 22". Large shelf is cushion height. ($250-300)

M 908 G – Step-End Table (1954-55) Top measures 16" x 15". Shelf is 30" x 16". Height 22 ½". ($375-475)

CM 974 G – Step-End Table (Aristocraft, 1954-55) The shelf of this tier table is 28" x 15". Overall height 22". Large shelf is cushion height. ($250-275)

M 1154 G – Step-End Table (1955-56) Top measures 20" x 19". Shelf is 28" x 17". Height 22". ($225-275)

M 1164 G – Step-End Table (1956-59) Top measures 14" x 20". Shelf is 30" x 20". Height 22". ($150-200)

M 1574 G – Step-End Table (1956-58) Top measures 15" x 18". Shelf is 30" x 18". Height 22". Also available with plastic top and shelf—order as M 1574 GP. ($200-250)

CM 1704 G – Step-End Table (Aristocraft, 1958) Top measures 14" x 15". Shelf is 28" x 15". Overall height 21". ($200-250)

M 1584 G – Step-End Table (1956) Top measures 17" x 16 ½". Shelf is 30" x 20". Height 22 ½". ($400-450)

Corner Tables

M 338 G – Corner Table (1950-54) Top measures 32" x 32". Height 21 ½". The shelf is 32" x 32" cushion height. ($450-550)

M 1504 G – Step-End Table (1957-63) Top measures 20" wide by 15" long. The shelf is 30" long by 20" wide. Shelf height 15". Overall height 21". ($275-350)

M 339 G – Corner Table (1950) The shaped and moulded top is supported by a flush, steam-bent rim. The lower shelf is cushion height. The solid wood top measures 32" square. Height 22". ($550-650)

CM 370 G – Corner Table (Aristocraft, 1950-54) The cut-back top of this corner table permits full use of the 30" x 30" shelf. The tiered top has the same overall dimensions. Height overall 21". Shelf is cushion high. ($400-500)

M 1140 G – Corner Table (1955-56) Top measures 36" x 36". Cushion height shelf is 40" x 40". Overall size 42" x 42". Height 23". ($250-350)

CM 970 G – Corner Table (Aristocraft, 1954-55) The cut-back top of this corner table permits full use of the 30" x 30" shelf. Height overall 23". Shelf is cushion high. ($400-450)

M 1570 G – Corner Table (1956) Top measures 30" x 30". Cushion high shelf is 30" x 30". Overall 32 ¼" x 32 ¼". Height 22". Also available with plastic top and shelf—order as M 1570 GP. ($250-300)

M 938 G – Corner Table (1954-55) The top measures 32" x 32". The cushion-high shelf (16" high) is the same size. Height 24". ($500-575)

M 1590 G – Corner Table (1956-57) Top measures 34" x 34". Cushion high shelf is 29" x 29". Height 22". ($375-450)

M 1150 G – Corner Table (1957-59) Top measures 33" x 33". Cushion high shelf is 33" square. Height 22". ($250-350)

M 1507 G – Corner Table (1957-63) Top measures 31" wide by 31" deep. The shelf is 32" square. Shelf height is 15". Overall height 21". ($375-450)

CM 1707 G – Corner Table (Aristocraft, 1958) Top measures 30" x 30". Shelf is 30" x 30". Overall height 21". ($250-350)

Other Tables

M 312 G – Nest of Tables (1950-54) The largest table of this group has a 21" x 15" top. It stands 24" high. The middle one has a 19" x 13 ½" top and is 23" high. The smallest one has a 17" x 12" top and stands 22" high. ($700-800)

M 393 G – Center Table (1950-52) This utility table can be used as a lamp table, picture window unit, or as a high corner table. Fitted with 3-legged pedestal base. Top is 30" in diameter. Height 26". ($800-900)

M 396 G – Wedge-Shaped Tier Table (1950-54) This table is especially designed to permit curved arrangements with regular seating units. Used between fillers, left and right sectional pieces, and chairs, this table is ideal for curved television arrangements. Size of cushion height shelf 22" at back and 12" at front. Length 30". Overall height 22". ($375-450)

M 902 G – Nest of Tables (1954-55) All tops are same size: 19 ½" deep x 27" wide. Heights are 24", 21 ¾", 19 ½". ($1,250-1,500)

M 1587 G – Drop-Leaf Utility Table (1956-58) Size of top with both leaves up as shown, 42" in diameter; with both leaves down, 42" x 19 ½". Height 24". ($550-650)

In 1954, the first "TV dinner" was marketed by the Swanson company and was an immediate hit with the American public. Recognizing this new penchant for eating in the living room, Heywood-Wakefield introduced its M 1587 G Drop-Leaf Utility Table in 1956, noting its "new height" prominently in the catalog. "Conventional cocktail tables (16" or 17" high) are too low and dining tables (29" high) are too high for use with low upholstered living room chairs for eating purposes. The M 1587 G table (24" high) is exactly the right height for dining when seated in upholstered living room chairs, etc." In keeping with Heywood-Wakefield's emphasis on versatility, the catalog goes on to note that the M 1587 G table can also be used as a TV table, a corner table, a picture window unit, a foyer table (with the leaves down), or a wall table.

Desks

M 314 W – Student's Desk (1950-52) Finished in back with solid wood, not veneer. Adjustable shelf at right. Full length top drawer and deep file drawer at left. Top measures 44" x 22". Height 30". ($1,150-1,350)

In addition to the desks shown here, many of the vanities shown in the Bedroom section could also be used as desks—and were often shown that way in catalogs. The company emphasized that most desks and vanities were fully finished on the rear, so they did not need to be placed against a wall.

M 320 W – Kneehole Desk (1950-59) Finished in back with solid wood, not veneer. Steam-bent drawer fronts. Deep file drawer on left. Top measures 50" x 24". Height 30". ($1,750-2,000)

M 315 W – Kneehole Desk (1950) Has a finished back so that it can be placed anywhere in the room. It has six drawers including the long, full length top drawer and a double, deep, file drawer on the left. The top measures 50" x 24". It stands 30" high. ($1,750-2,000)

M 327 W – Table Desk (1950-55) This table desk can be used as a server, dressing table, foyer piece, or as a desk. Top measures 40" x 20". Height 30". ($900-1,000)

M 389 W – Desk Chest (1952-55) Top measures 30" x 13". Height 42". ($1,250-1,500)

M 783 W – Student's Desk (1952-61) Finished in back with solid wood, not veneer. Full length top drawer and file drawer at left. Top measures 44" x 22". Height 30". ($1,150-1,350)

M 934 W – Starter Chest with Desk Drawer (1954) Fitted with desk drawer at top. Top measures 32" x 18". Height 32 ½", which is same height as bookcases, many utility cabinets, etc. ($1,150-1,300)

M 1923 – Corner Desk (1958-59) Fitted with one drawer. Top measures 31" x 31". Height is 30". ($375-475)

Bookcases

M 322 – **Corner Bookcase** (1950-61) Top measures 28" x 11". Height 32 ½". Fitted with two adjustable shelves. ($800-950)

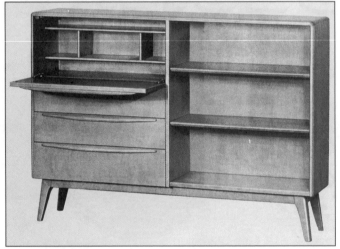

M 328 W – **Desk Bookcase** (1950-55) This large utility wall piece is especially useful as a storage unit. Fitted with three drawers and adjustable bookcase shelves. Front panel door forms desk writing surface 29" high. "Pigeon-hole" desk section is adjustable for height and is removable for added storage space. Size of top 60" wide x 13" deep. Overall height 42" ($1,700-2,000)

M 326 – **Cabinet Bookcase** (1952–61) Fitted with an adjustable shelf inside cabinet doors. Top measures 36" x 11". Height 32 ½". ($800-950)

M 321 – **Straight Bookcase** (1950-63) Fitted with two adjustable shelves. Top measures 36" x 11". Height 32 ½". ($650-750)

M 1921 – Straight Bookcase (1958-59) Fitted with adjustable shelf. Top measures 36" x 12". Height is 30". ($300-400)

M 1922 – Corner Bookcase (1958-59) Fitted with adjustable shelf. Top measures 24" x 24". Height is 30". ($375-475)

M 179 – Tambour Utility Case (1950-55) This tambour front case is 32 ½" high to fit in with sectional bookcase units. Fitted with an adjustable shelf inside. Roomy enough for small radio, record player, and records. Top measures 24" x 17". ($1,200-1,300)

M 523 – Utility Case (1950-55) Top measures 30" x 19" deep. Height 34". A pair of these cases forms an extra wide Mr. and Mrs. dresser arrangement. ($800-950)

M 505 on M 504 – Room Divider (1953-56) Living room side of the Room Divider is shown above. Dining room side is shown at left. Base is 60" wide, 18 ½" deep, and 30" high. Top section measures 60" wide, 11" deep, and 30" high. Overall height is 60". ($3,000-3,300)

M 534 – Utility Cabinet (1950-54) Useful as a server, china base, dresser, or living room piece. Grain runs horizontal on sides to eliminate sticky or loose drawers with temperature changes. Center drawer guides. Top measures 34" x 15 ½". Height 32 ½". ($800-950)

M 528 – Pier Cabinet (1952-55) Ideal for sectional wall arrangements or as night table and bedroom piece where wall space is limited. Top measures 18" x 15 ½". Height 32 ½". ($800-950)

M 1924 – Wall Cabinet (1958-59) Fitted with two doors and one adjustable shelf. Top measures 24" x 24". Height is 30". ($300-400)

M 1925 – Corner Cabinet (1958-59) Fitted with door and adjustable shelf. Top measures 24" x 24". Height is 30". ($300-400)

114

Dining Rooms

As noted previously, Heywood-Wakefield stressed flexibility as one of the hallmarks of Modern furniture. For the dining room, flexibility was largely achieved through a wide assortment of dining tables—including oblong extension, round extension, pedestal, and drop leaf—suited for many different size homes or apartments. Note that some dining room groups were produced in the same design motifs as those used for the company's bedroom suites. For example, the Harmonic server (M 996), china (M 995), and buffets (M 997 and M 998) were intended to be used with or without the corresponding Harmonic bedroom pieces. Similarly, the Cadence dining room pieces (M 1125 through M 1135 G) shared the same design elements as the Cadence bedroom suite, but could of course be used independently.

1930s and 1940s – The Streamline Years

C 2687 A – Side Chair (1935-37) Seat 18" x 16 ½". Height of back 15". *Available* in Walma, Amber, Bleached, Modern Walnut. ($250-350)

C 2683 G – Combination Game and Dinette Table (1935) Woods—Quilted Maple and Plain Striped Walnut. Fitted with sliding refectory and leaves. Size of top—open 48" x 30", closed 30" x 30". Height 29". *Finish*—Walma. ($850-1,000)

C 2697 C – Chromium Frame Arm Chair (1935) Width of seat 17 ½". Depth of seat 23". Height of back 16". ($900-1,000)

C 2670 G – Coffee Table (1935-36) Woods—Quilted Maple and Plain Striped Walnut. Length 30". Width 17". Height 16". *Finish*—Walma. ($700-800)

C 2686 – China or Utility Case (1935) Woods—Quilted Maple and Plain Striped Walnut. Fitted with adjustable shelves. Entire right hand side of piece is storage compartment. Length 36". Width 15". Height 51". *Finish*—Walma. ($1,150-1,300)

C 2687 A – Side Chair (1935-37) Seat 18" x 16 ½". Height of back 15". *Available* in Walma, Amber, Bleached, Modern Walnut. ($250-350)

C 2688 G – Combination Dining and Console Table (1935) Top folds lengthwise to form console table. Size of top open 50" x 46". Folded 50" x 23". Height of table 29". Woods—Quilted Maple and Plain Striped Walnut. *Finish*—Walma. ($1,200-1,500)

C 2685 – Buffet or Utility Cabinet (1935) Woods—Quilted Maple and Plain Striped Walnut. Lower section has two doors. Inside fitted with adjustable shelves. Upper half-tier is silver drawer. Length 45". Width 15". Height 42". *Finish*—Walma. ($1,150-1,300)

C 2689 – Dinette Buffet Server (1935) Length 32". Width 15". Height 32". *Finishes*—Honey and Green, Honey and Red, Maple and Green, Maple and Red; two-tone combination Walnut. ($800-1,000)

C 2676 A – Side Chair (1935) Fluted backs. Wood—Birch. Seat 16" x 15 ½". Height of back 15". *Finishes*—Honey and Green, Honey and Red, Maple and Green, Maple and Red; two-tone Walnut combination. ($200-275)

C 2677 G – Extension Dinette Table (1935) Fluted corners. Wood—Birch. Size of top open 50" x 30". Top closed 40" x 30". Height 29". *Finishes*—Honey and Green, Honey and Red; Maple and Green, Maple and Red; two-tone Walnut combination. ($750-1,000)

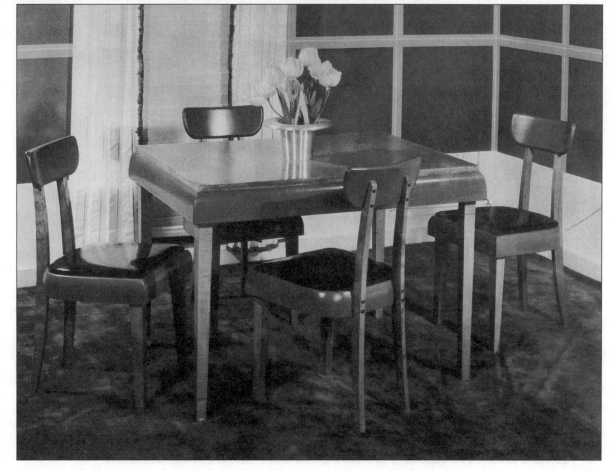

C 2668 G – Extension Dinette Table (1935) Wood—Birch. Top open 50" x 30". Top closed 40" x 30". Height 29". *Finishes*—Honey and Green; Honey and Red; Maple and Green, Maple and Red; two-tone Walnut combination. ($650-800)

C 2669 A – Side Chair (1935) Wood—Birch. Seat 14 ½" x 14 ½". Height of back 14 ½". *Finishes*—Honey and Green, Honey and Red, Maple and Green, Maple and Red; two-tone Walnut combination. ($175-225)

117

C 2794 C – Arm Chair
(1936-40) Seat 19" x 17".
Height of back 17". *Available*
in Wheat, Champagne,
Amber, Bleached, or Modern
Walnut. *Designed by Gilbert
Rhode.* ($650-750)

C 2794 A – Side Chair
(1936) Seat 15 ½" x 14 ½".
Height of back 16 ½".
Available in Wheat,
Champagne, Amber,
Bleached, or Modern Walnut.
Designed by Gilbert Rhode.
($550-650)

**C 2932 G – Extension
Dining Table** (1936-39) Size
of top open 42" x 84". Size of
top closed 42" x 60". Fitted
with two leaves. Height 29".
Available in Wheat,
Champagne, Amber, or
Bleached. ($2,500-3,000)

C 2914-L – Left Pier Cabinet
(1936-37) Top 16" x 19".
Height 34". *Available* in
Amber or Bleached. ($550-
650)

C 2910 – Center Cabinet
(1936-37) May be used in
bedroom groupings or as the
center section of a three piece
buffet. Size of top 32" x 19".
Height 34". *Available* in
Amber, Bleached, combina-
tion of Amber and Bleached.
($900-1,000)

C 2915-R – Right Pier Cabinet (1936-37) Top 16" x 19". Height 34". *Available* in Amber or Bleached. ($550-650)

C 2912 – Hutch-shelf (1936-37) This piece may be used on the C 2917 Server to form a dining hutch or on the C 2911 W to form a secretary. Size 31" x 11". Height 24". *Available* in Amber or Bleached. ($300-400)

C 2917 – Server (1937) Size of top 32" x 15 ½". Height 32 ½". *Available* in Amber or Bleached. ($500-700)

C 2916 A – Side Chair (1936) Seat 16" x 15 ½". Height of back 14 ½". *Available* in Amber or Bleached. ($125-150)

C 2916 G – Extension Table (1936-37) Size of top open 30" x 50". Size of top closed 30" x 40". Height 29". *Available* in Amber or Bleached. ($500-600)

C 2917 – Server (1937) Size of top 32" x 15 ½". Height 32 ½". *Available* in Amber or Bleached. ($500-700)

C 2913 – Closed Cabinet (1936-37) This piece may be used on the C 2917 Server to form a closed dining hutch or on the C 2910 to form a chest on chest for bedroom use. Size 31" x 14". Height 17". *Available* in Amber or Bleached. ($375-475)

C 2918 C – Arm Chair (1936-37) Seat 16 ½" x 17". Height of back 15 ½". *Available* in Amber or Bleached. ($650-750)

C 2918 A – Side Chair (1936-37) Seat 16 ½" x 17". Height of back 15 ½". *Available* in Amber or Bleached. ($500-600)

C 2918 G – Swing-leaf Table (1936-38) The two end leaves of this table swing flat under the top when not in use. Size of top with leaves extended 32" x 68". Size of top with leaves folded under 32" x 48". Height 29". *Available* in Wheat, Amber, or Bleached. ($1,350-1,500)

C 2914-L – Left Pier Cabinet (1936-37) Top 16" x 19". Height 34". *Available* in Amber or Bleached. ($550-650)

C 2910 – Center Cabinet (1936-37) May be used in bedroom groupings or as the center section of a three piece buffet. Size of top 32" x 19". Height 34". *Available* in Amber, Bleached, combination of Amber and Bleached. ($900-1,000)

C 2915-R – Right Pier Cabinet (1936-37) Top 16" x 19". Height 34". *Available* in Amber or Bleached. ($550-650)

C 2912 – Hutch-shelf (1936-37) This piece may be used on the C 2917 Server to form a dining hutch or on the C 2911 W to form a secretary. Size 31" x 11". Height 24". *Available* in Amber or Bleached. ($300-400)

C 2917 – Server (1937) Size of top 32" x 15 ½". Height 32 ½". *Available* in Amber or Bleached. ($500-700)

C 2932 G – Extension Dining Table (1936-39) Size of top open 42" x 84". Size of top closed 42" x 60". Fitted with two leaves. Height 29". *Available* in Wheat, Champagne, Amber, or Bleached. ($2,500-3,000)

C 3346 A – Side Chair (1937-39) Seat 16 ½" x 16 ½". Height of back 16". *Available* in Wheat, Champagne, Amber, Bleached, or Modern Walnut. ($300-350)

C 3346 C – Arm Chair (1937-39) Seat 16 ½" x 16 ½". Height of back 16". *Available* in Wheat, Champagne, Amber, Bleached, or Modern Walnut. ($375-425)

C 3318 – Buffet (1937-39) Long, bottom drawer accommodates large size table linen with a minimum of folding. Fitted with silver drawer. Size of top 52" x 19". Height 34". *Available* in Wheat, Champagne, Amber, or Bleached. ($1,250-1,500)

C 3316 – China Top (1937-39) This piece may be used with the C 3317 Server to form a China. Fitted with two adjustable shelves. *Available* in Wheat, Champagne, Amber, or Bleached. ($450-500)

C 3317 – Server or China Base (1937-39) This piece may be used alone as a Server or with the C 3316 China Top to form a China. Size of top 32" x 18". Height 30". *Available* in Wheat, Champagne, Amber, or Bleached. ($1,050-1,200)

C 2918 G – Swing-leaf Table (1936-38) The two end leaves of this table swing flat under the top when not in use. Size of top with leaves extended 32" x 68". Size of top with leaves folded under 32" x 48". Height 29". *Available* in Wheat, Amber, or Bleached. ($1,350-1,500)

C 2794 A – Side Chair (1936) Seat 15 ½" x 14 ½". Height of back 16 ½". *Available* in Wheat, Champagne, Amber, Bleached, or Modern Walnut. ($550-650)

C 2794 C – Arm Chair (1936-40) Seat 19" x 17". Height of back 17". *Available* in Wheat, Champagne, Amber, Bleached, or Modern Walnut. ($650-750)

C 3312 – Hutch-Shelf (1937-39) This piece may be used with the C 3310 chest to form an open shelf hutch buffet; with the C 3311 W Desk-Chest to form a Secretary Desk; or with the C 3314 Server to form a dining hutch. Size 31" x 11". Height 25". *Available* in Wheat, Champagne, Amber, or Bleached. ($400-500)

C 3314 – Server (1937-38) The C 3314 Server may be used with the C 3312 (open hutch shelf) to form an open dining hutch. Size of top 32" x 15 ½". Height 32 ½". *Available* in Wheat, Amber, or Bleached. ($650-850)

C 3180 G – Extension Table (1937) Size of top open 30" x 50". Size of top closed 30" x 40". Height 29". *Available* in Amber or Bleached. ($500-600)

C 3180 A – Side Chair (1937) Seat 16" x 15". Height of back 15". *Available* in Amber or Bleached. ($125-150)

C 3312 – Hutch-Shelf (1937-39) This piece may be used with the C 3310 chest to form an open shelf hutch buffet; with the C 3311 W Desk-Chest to form a Secretary Desk; or with the C 3314 Server to form a dining hutch. Size 31" x 11". Height 25". *Available* in Wheat, Champagne, Amber, or Bleached. ($375-475)

C 3310 – 4-Drawer Chest (1937-39) This piece may be used as an extra 4-drawer Chest for the C 3300 suite or with the C 3312 to form an open shelf hutch buffet. Size of top 32" x 19". Height 34". *Available* in Wheat, Champagne, Amber, or Bleached. ($650-750)

C 2925 G – Console or Game Table (1936-38) The top of this table folds and pivots. It serves as a small wall table; as a console table; or, with the top turned, as a game table. Size of top open 32" square; folded 32" x 16". Height 28". *Available* in Wheat, Amber, or Bleached. ($900-1,000)

C 2918 G – Swing-leaf Table
(1936-38) The two end leaves of
this table swing flat under the
top when not in use. Size of top
with leaves extended 32" x 68".
Size of top with leaves folded
under 32" x 48". Height 29".
Available in Wheat, Amber, or
Bleached. ($1,350-1,500)

C 3324 AX – Side Chair (1937-
38) Seat 16" x 14". Height of
back 16 ½". *Available* in Wheat,
Amber, Bleached, or Modern
Walnut. ($550-650)

C 3324 CX – Arm Chair (1937-
38) Seat 16" x 14". Height of
back 16 ½". *Available* in Wheat,
Amber, Bleached, or Modern
Walnut. ($650-750)

C 3313 – Closed Cabinet
(1937) This piece may be used
on the C 3314 Server to form a
closed dining hutch. Size 31" x
11 ¾". Height 24". *Available* in
Amber or Bleached. ($375-475)

C 3314 – Server (1937-38) The
C 3314 Server may be used with
the C 3312 open hutch shelf to
form a dining hutch or with the
C 3313 to form a closed dining
hutch. Size of top 32" x 15 ½".
Height 32 ½". Available in
Wheat, Amber, or Bleached.
($650-850)

C 3315 – Buffet (1937-38) Size of top 45" x 18". Height 34". *Available* in Wheat, Amber, or Bleached. ($1,550-1,800)

**C 3319 G – Extension
Table** (1937-39) Fitted
with one leaf. Size of
top open 30" x 50".
Size of top closed 30"
x 40". Height 29".
Available in Wheat,
Champagne, Amber, or
Bleached. ($500-600)

**C 3322 A – Side
Chair** (1937-39) Seat
16 ½" x 15". Height of
back 16". *Available* in
Wheat, Champagne,
Amber, or Bleached.
($125-150)

**C 3317 – Server or
China Base** (1937-39)
This piece may be
used alone as a Server
or with the C 3316
China Top to form a
China. Size of top 32" x
18". Height 30".
Available in Wheat,
Champagne, Amber, or
Bleached. ($1,050-
1,200)

C 3319 G – Extension Table (1937-39) Fitted with one leaf. Size of top open 30" x 50". Size of top closed 30" x 40". Height 29". *Available* in Wheat, Champagne, Amber, or Bleached. ($500-600)

C 3321 A – Side Chair (1937-39) Seat 16 ½" x 16 ½". Height of back 15". *Available* in Wheat, Amber, or Bleached. ($100-125)

C 3347 G – Extension Table (1938-39) Fitted with two extension leaves. Size of top open 36" x 76". Size of top closed 36" x 54". Height 29". *Available* in Wheat, Champagne, Amber, or Bleached. ($2,200-2,500)

C 3314 – Server (1937-38) The C 3314 Server may be used with the C 3312 open hutch shelf to form a dining hutch or with the C 3313 to form a closed dining hutch. Size of top 32" x 15 ½". Height 32 ½". Available in Wheat, Amber, or Bleached. ($650-850)

C 3324 AX – Side Chair (1937-38) Seat 16" x 14". Height of back 16 ½". *Available* in Wheat, Amber, Bleached, or Modern Walnut. ($550-650)

C 3324 CX – Arm Chair (1937-38) Seat 16" x 14". Height of back 16 ½". *Available* in Wheat, Amber, Bleached, or Modern Walnut. ($650-750)

C 3315 – Buffet (1937-38) Size of top 45" x 18". Height 34". *Available* in Wheat, Amber, or Bleached. ($1,550-1,800)

C 3349 G – Gate-Leg Table (1938-40) A popular Gate-leg Dining Table with a multitude of uses in the modern home. The top measures 36" x 60" with both drop leaves extended. With one leaf up, it is 36" square. With both leaves down, the top measures 36" x 13 ¾" and may readily serve as a console, wall or ball table. Height 29". *Available* in Wheat, Champagne, Amber, or Bleached. ($650-850)

C 3322 A – Side Chair (1937-39) Seat 16 ½" x 15". Height of back 16". *Available* in Wheat, Champagne, Amber, or Bleached. ($125-150)

C 3317 – Server or China Base (1937-39) This piece may be used alone as a Server or with the C 3316 China Top to form a China. Size of top 32" x 18". Height 30". *Available* in Wheat, Champagne, Amber, or Bleached. ($1,050-1,200)

Heywood-Wakefield described this grouping and the one in the next picture as "Swedish Modern" in design.

C 3361 G – Extension Table (1938-39) Fitted with one leaf. Size of top open 30" x 50". Size of top closed 30" x 40". Height 29". *Available* in Wheat, Champagne, Amber, or Bleached. ($650-750)

C 3361 A – Side Chair (1938-39) Seat 16" x 15". Height of back 16". *Available* in Wheat, Champagne, Amber, or Bleached. ($125-150)

C 3348 – Corner Cabinet (1938-39) Equally adaptable to the dining room or the living room of the modern home. It measures 14 ½" deep; 24" wide; and 65" high. Lower closed compartment fitted with shelf. *Available* in Wheat, Champagne, Amber, or Bleached. ($1,200-1,400)

C 3312 – Hutch-Shelf (1937-39) This piece may be used with the C 3310 chest to form an open shelf hutch buffet; with the C 3311 W Desk-Chest to form a Secretary Desk; or with the C 3314 Server to form a dining hutch. Size 31" x 11". Height 25". *Available* in Wheat, Champagne, Amber, or Bleached. ($400-500)

C 3310 – 4-Drawer Chest (1937-39) This piece may be used as an extra 4-drawer Chest for the C 3300 suite or with the C 3312 to form an open shelf hutch buffet. Size of top 32" x 19". Height 34". *Available* in Wheat, Champagne, Amber, or Bleached. ($650-750)

C 3361 G – Extension Table (1938-39) Fitted with one leaf. Size of top open 30" x 50". Size of top closed 30" x 40". Height 29". *Available* in Wheat, Champagne, Amber, or Bleached. ($650-750)

C 3363 A – Side Chair (1938-39) Seat 16 ½" x 15 ½". Height of back 15". *Available* in Wheat. ($125-150)

C 3362 – Buffet (1938-39) Size of top 48" x 18". Height 35". *Available* in Wheat, Champagne, Amber, or Bleached. ($900-1,200)

C 2925 G – Console or Game Table (1936-38) The top of this table folds and pivots. It serves as a small wall table; as a console table; or, with the top turned, as a game table. Size of top open 32" square; folded 32" x 16". Height 28". *Available* in Wheat, Amber, or Bleached. ($900-1,000)

C 2932 G – Extension Dining Table (1936-39) Size of top open 42" x 84". Size of top closed 42" x 60". Fitted with two leaves. Height 29". *Available* in Wheat, Champagne, Amber, or Bleached. ($2,500-3,000)

C 3535 A – Side Chair (1939-43) Seat 16" x 16 ½". Height of back 17". *Available* in Wheat, Champagne, Amber, or Bleached. *Designed by Count Sakhnoffsky.* ($375-475)

C 3535 C – Arm Chair (1939-43) Width between arms 17 ½". Depth of seat 16 ½". Height of back 17". *Available* in Wheat, Champagne, Amber, or Bleached. *Designed by Count Sakhnoffsky.* ($450-550)

C 3318 – Buffet (1937-39) Long, bottom drawer accommodates large size table linen. Fitted with silver drawer. Size of top 52" x 19". Height 34". *Available* in Wheat, Champagne, Amber, or Bleached. ($1,250-1,500)

C 3317 – Server or China Base (1937-39) This piece may be used alone as a Server or with the C 3316 China Top to form a China. Size of top 32" x 18". Height 30". *Available* in Wheat, Champagne, Amber, or Bleached. ($1,050-1,200)

C 2932 G – Extension Dining Table (1936-39) Size of top open 42" x 84". Size of top closed 42" x 60". Fitted with two leaves. Height 29". *Available* in Wheat, Champagne, Amber, or Bleached. ($2,500-3,000)

C 3530 A – Side Chair (1939-42) Width of seat 18". Depth of seat 17". Height of back 16". *Available* in Wheat, Champagne, Amber, or Bleached. ($175-250)

C 3530 C – Arm Chair (1939-42) Width of seat 18". Depth of seat 17". Height of back 16". *Available* in Wheat, Champagne, Amber, or Bleached. ($200-250)

C 3318 – Buffet (1937-39) Long, bottom drawer accommodates large size table linen. Size of top 52" x 19". Height 34". *Available* in Wheat, Champagne, Amber, or Bleached. ($1,250-1,500)

C 3316 – China Top (1937-39) This piece may be used with the C 3317 Server to form a China. Fitted with two adjustable shelves. *Available* in Wheat, Champagne, Amber, or Bleached. ($450-500)

C 3317 – Server or China Base (1937-39) This piece may be used alone as a Server or with the C 3316 China Top to form a China. Size of top 32" x 18". Height 30". *Available* in Wheat, Champagne, Amber, or Bleached. ($1,050-1,200)

C 3537 G – Extension Table (1939) Size of top closed 30" x 40". Top open 30" x 50". Fitted with one leaf. Height 29". *Available* in Wheat, Champagne, Amber, or Bleached. ($800-1,000)

C 3536 A – Side Chair (1939-40) Seat 16 ½" x 15 ½". Height of back 15 ½". *Available* in Wheat, Champagne, Amber, or Bleached. ($150-200)

C 3362 – Buffet (1938-39) Size of top 48" x 18". Height 35". *Available* in Wheat, Champagne, Amber, or Bleached. ($900-1,200)

As noted on page 31, the "Textured Modern" ensemble of living room, dining room, and bedroom pieces was found only in a small 1939 brochure with no accompanying price list or other documentation. They may have been manufactured for a brief time only or perhaps not at all.

C 3511 A – Side Chair (1939) ($75-100)

C 3511 C – Arm Chair (1939) ($100-125)

C 3512 G – Extension Table (1939) Top opens to 76" x 34". ($500-600)

C 3517 – Buffet (1939) Has three center drawers and two end storage compartments. The top measures 46" x 18". ($450-550)

This small dinette set was also part of the "Textured Modern" ensemble.

C 3510 G – Extension Table (1939) Opens to 30" x 50". ($400-500)

C 3510 A – Side Chair (1939) ($75-100)

C 3515 – Server (1939) Top measures 32" x 16". Height 30". ($350-450)

C 3707 G – **Extension Table** (1940-42) Size of top closed, 42" x 60"; open 42" x 84". Fitted with 2 leaves. Height 29". ($1,250-1,500)

C 3530 A – **Side Chair** (1939-42) Seat 18" x 17". Height of back 16". ($175-250)

C 3530 C – **Arm Chair** (1939-42) Seat 18" x 17". Height of back 16". ($200-250)

C 3708 – **Buffet** (1940-42) Long, bottom drawer accommodates large size table linen with a minimum of folding. Fitted with silver drawer. Size of top 52" x 19". Height 35". ($1,150-1,250)

C 3711 – **China Top** (1940) Top shelf is adjustable. 28" long, 12" deep, 31" high. ($375-475)

C 3710 – **Server** (1940-44) Top 32" x 18" top. Height 30". ($650-750)

C 3706 G – **Extension Table** (1940) Size of top open, 38" x 76"; closed 38" x 54". Fitted with 2 leaves. Height 29". ($1,250-1,500)

C 3701 A – **Side Chair** (1940) Seat 16" x 15". Height of back 16". ($175-200)

C 3701 C – **Arm Chair** (1940) Seat 16" x 15". Height of back 16". ($200-225)

C 3708 – **Buffet** (1940-42) Long, bottom drawer accommodates large size table linen with a minimum of folding. Fitted with silver drawer. Size of top 52" x 19". Height 35". ($1,150-1,400)

C 3389 G – **Console or Game Table** (1939-42) Top of this table folds and pivots...serves as small wall table, as a console table, or, with the top turned, as a card table. Size of top open, 32" square, folded 32" x 16". Height 28". ($950-1,000)

C 3716 G – **Console Extension Table** (1940) A practical, all-purpose table for console, dinette, or dining room use. Completely closed top measures 38" wide x 20" deep. Height 30". When fully extended, top measures 38" x 76". Height 29". Fitted with three leaves and drop-leg attachment for center of table when fully extended. ($900-1,200)

C 3726 – **Kneehole Desk** (1940-42) Size of top 44" x 18". Height 30". Fitted with plastic pulls. ($650-750)

C 2794 A – **Side Chair** (1936) Seat 15 ½" x 14 ½". Height of back 16 ½". ($550-650)

C 2794 C 4CB – **Channel Back Arm Chair** (1938-40) Seat 19" x 17". Height of back 17". Upholstered with 4 channels on back. ($650-750)

C 3705 G – **Tea Table** (1940-42) May be used as tea, dinette, card, or corner table. Top is 30" square. Height 29". ($900-1,000)

C 3715 A – **Side Chair** (1940-42) Seat 16" x 15". Height of back 16 ½". ($125-150)

C 3594 G – Extension Table (1940) Fitted with one extension leaf. Size of top open 34" x 64"; closed, 34" x 50". Height 29". ($750-1,000)

C 3596 A – Side Chair (1940-44) Seat 16" x 16". Height of back 16". ($200-225)

C 3596 C – Arm Chair (1940-44) Width between arms 18". Depth of seat 16". Height of back 16". ($225-250)

C 3709 – Buffet (1940-42) Size of top 48" x 18". Height 35". ($1,550-1,800)

C 3389 G – Console or Game Table (1939-42) Top of this table folds and pivots…serves as a small wall table, as a console table, or, with the top turned, as a card table. Size of top open, 32" square; folded, 32" x 16". Height 28". ($950-1,000)

C 3704 G – Extension Table (1940-42) Fitted with one extension leaf. Size of top open, 32" x 56"; closed, 32" x 46". Height 29". ($1,000-1,100)

C 3702 A – Side Chair (1940-42) Seat 16" x 15". Height of back 16". ($100-125)

C 3702 C – Arm Chair (1940-42) Seat 16" x 15". Height of back 16". ($125-150)

C 3585 – Hutch Top (1940) Shelf is adjustable. 30 ½" wide, 24" high, 10 ¼" deep. ($250-400)

C 3583 – Cabinet Base (1940) 32" wide, 13 ¾" deep, 32 ½" high. ($900-1,000)

C 3713 G – Extension Table (1940) Fitted with one extension leaf. Size of top open 30" x 50"; closed 30" x 40". ($850-1,000)

C 3595 A – Side Chair (1940-44) Seat 16" x 17". Height of back 16". ($150-200)

C 3595 C – Arm Chair (1940-44) Width between arms 18". Depth of seat 17". Height of back 16". ($175-200)

C 3709 – Buffet (1940-42) Size of top 48" x 18". Height 35". ($1,550-1,800)

C 3713 G – Extension Table (1940) Fitted with one extension leaf. Size of top open, 30" x 50"; closed 30" x 40". ($850-1,000)

C 3536 A – Side Chair (1939-40) Seat 16 ½" x 15 ½". Height of back 15 ½". ($150-200)

C 3585 – Hutch Top (1940) Hutch shelf is adjustable. 30 ½" wide, 24" high, 10 ¼" deep. ($250-400)

C 3584 – Chest Base (1940) 32" wide, 17" deep, 34" high. ($1,000-1,100)

C 3389 G – Console or Game Table (1939-42) Top of this table folds and pivots…serves as a small wall table, as a console table, or, with the top turned, as a card table. Size of top open, 32" square; folded, 32" x 16". Height 28". ($950-1,000)

131

C 3703 G – Extension Table (1940) Fitted with one extension leaf. Size of top open, 30" x 50"; closed, 30" x 40". Height 29". ($500-600)

C 3714 A – Side Chair (1940-42) Seat 16" x 15". Height of back 16". ($125-150)

C 3583 – Cabinet Base (1940) Size of top 32" x 13 ¾". Height 32 ½". ($900-1,000)

C 3703 G – Extension Table (1940) Fitted with one extension leaf. Size of top open, 30" x 50"; closed, 30" x 40". Height 29". ($500-600)

C 3700 A – Side Chair (1940-44) Seat 16" x 15". Height of back 18". ($125-150)

C 3710 – Server (1940-44) Size of top 32" x 18". Height 30". ($650-750)

C 3712 G – Extension Table (1940) Fitted with one extension leaf. Size of top open, 30" x 50"; closed, 30" x 40". Height of table 29". ($500-600)

C 3588 A – Side Chair (1940) Seat 16" x 15". Height of back 16". ($125-150)

C 3348 X – Corner Cabinet (1940-43) This corner cabinet is equally adaptable to the dining room or living room. It measures 24" wide, 14 ½" deep, and 65" high. Lower, closed compartment is fitted with shelf. ($1,200-1,400)

C 3958 G – Drop-Leaf Extension Table (1941-42) Size of top fully extended and with both extension leaves in, 38" x 78". Size with no leaves in but with end drop-leaves up, 38" x 54". Size of top with end drop-leaves down, 38" x 24". Height 29". ($750-900)

C 3596 A – Side Chair (1940-44) Seat 16" x 16". Height of back 16". ($200-225)

C 3596 C – Arm Chair (1940-44) Width between arms 18". Depth of seat 16". Height of back 16". ($225-250)

C 3585 – Hutch Top (1940) Top shelf is adjustable. 30 ½" wide, 24" high, 10 ¼" deep. ($250-400)

C 3975 – Chest (1941-42) 4-drawer chest. 32" x 17" top, 34" high. ($800-1,000)

C 3957 G – Gate-Leg Table (1941-42)
Dual purpose design for dining-living-foyer
or console use. Top measures 36" x 60" with
both drop leaves extended; with one leaf up
36" square, with both leaves down top
measures 36" x 14". ($800-1,000)

C 3951 A – Side Chair (1941-42) Seat 15
½" x 14 ½". Height of back 16 ½". ($300-
375)

**C 3941 G – Extension
Table** (1941-42) Fitted
with one 14" extension
leaf. Size of top open, 34"
x 64"; closed 34" x 50".
Height 29". ($800-1,000)

C 3940 A – Side Chair
(1941-42) Seat 16" x 15".
Height of back 16". ($175-
200)

C 3940 C – Arm Chair
(1941-42) Seat 16" x 15".
Height of back 16". ($200-
225)

**C 3711 X on C3710 –
China** (1941-44) This is
formed by using the C
3711 X, sliding glass-door
top ($375-475), on the C
3710 server base ($650-
750). Top shelf is
adjustable. C 3710 has a
32" x 18" top and is 30"
high. C 3711 X is 30"
long, 13" deep, and 34 ½"
high. Overall height of
china is 64 ½" high.

**C 3954 – Credenza
Buffet** (1941-44) Size of
top 48" x 19". Height 34"
Fitted with 3 center
drawers and two end
storage compartments.
($550-650)

134

C 3956 G – Extension Table (1941-44) Fitted with one 14" extension leaf. Size of top open, 34" x 64"; closed, 34" x 50". Height 29". ($800-1,000)

C 3953 A – Side Chair (1941-42) Seat 16" x 15". Height of back 16". ($200-225)

C 3953 C – Arm Chair (1941-42) Seat 16" x 15". Height of back 16". ($225-250)

C 3709 – Buffet (1940-42) Size of top 48" x 18". Height 35". ($1,550-1,800)

C 3711 X on C 3975 – China (1941-42) This is china shown in silhouette view below. It is formed by using the C 3711 X glass-door top ($375-475) on the C 3975 four-drawer base. ($800-1,000). Top shelf is adjustable. C 3975 has a 32" x 17" top and is 34" high. C 3711 X is 30" long, 13" deep, and 34 ½" high. Overall height of china is 68 ½" high.

C 3955 G – Extension Table (1941-42) Fitted with one extension leaf. Size of top open, 30" x 50"; closed, 30" x 40". Height 29". ($550-700)

C 3714 A – Side Chair (1940-42) Seat 16" x 15". Height of back 16". ($125-150)

C 3972 – Cabinet Server (1941-42) Size of top 32" x 13 ¾". Height 32 ½". ($800-1,000)

C 3940 G – Extension Table (1941-42) Fitted with one extension leaf. Size of top open, 30" x 50"; closed, 30" x 40". Height 29". ($800-1,000)

C 3952 A – Side Chair (1941-42) Seat 16 ½" x 15 ½". Height of back 16". ($175-200)

C 3975 – Chest (1941-42) This 4-drawer dining chest has a 32" x 17" top. It is 34" high. ($800-1,000)

C 3389 G – Console or Game Table (1939-42) Top of this table folds and pivots. Size of top open, 30" square; folded, 30" x 15". ($950-1,000)

C 3950 G – Extension Table (1941-43) Fitted with one extension leaf. Size of top open, 30" x 50"; closed, 30" x 40". Height 29". ($500-600)

C 3950 A – Side Chair (1941-43) Seat 16" x 15". Height of back 16". ($125-150)

C 3950 C – Arm Chair (1941-43) Size of seat 16" x 15". Height of back 16". ($150-175)

C 3348 X – Corner Cabinet (1940-43) This corner cabinet measures 24" wide, 14 ½" deep, and 65" high. Lower, closed compartment is fitted with shelf. ($1,200-1,400)

1950s – The Modern Years

M 161 G – **Dinette Extension Table** (1950) Top measures 42" x 32" closed, as shown. With a 12" leaf, the length goes to 54". Height 29". ($700-800)

C 3965 G – **Extension Table** (1943-44) Top closed measures 30" x 40". Fitted with leaf top, measures 30" x 50". ($500-600)

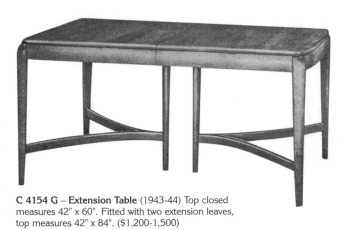

C 4154 G – **Extension Table** (1943-44) Top closed measures 42" x 60". Fitted with two extension leaves, top measures 42" x 84". ($1,200-1,500)

M 163 G – **Dining Extension Table** (1950) The table, as shown, is 50" long and 34" wide. Extended with one 14" leaf, it becomes 64" long, convenient for six guests. It stands 29" high. ($800-950)

M 165 G – Large Dining Extension Table (1950-53) Fitted with center leg and two 15" leaves. Top measures 60" x 42" closed; extends to 75" and 90". Height 29". ($1,550-1,800)

M 166 G – Drop-Leaf Dining Table (1950-55) Fitted with modern gatelegs. Top size, with both leaves down, 36" x 14"; with one leaf up, 36" x 37"; with both leaves up, 36" x 60". Height 29". ($900-1,000)

M 167 G – Drop-Leaf Extension Table (1950) This table is both a drop-leaf and an extension table. To the left it is used as a wall piece only 26" wide. Above, it is ready to serve 8 to 10 persons comfortably because of its 94" x 40" top. There are other sizes as well, depending upon how many 18" leaves are inserted and whether or not the drop leaves are used. At all lengths, the table is steadfastly rigid because of the 3 sets of pedestal legs. It stands 29" high. ($1,250-1,400)

M 169 G – Junior Dining Extension Table
(1950-55) Fitted with 14" leaf. Top measures
34" x 50" closed; 34" x 64" open. Height 29".
($800-1,000)

**M 313 G – Pivot-Top
Console Table** (1951-52)
Useful as a tea or game
table when fully opened up
to 32" x 32" size as shown
above. Space under top in
boxing is useful for storing
ashtrays, cards, coasters,
scorecards, and table
games. Size of top folded,
as shown at right, 32" x
16". Height 29". ($1,000-
1,100)

M 197 G – Pedestal Drop-Leaf Extension Table (1950-55) Butterfly supports
for drop-leaves keep table top level when extended; center legs offer added
rigidity at every table size. Fitted with two 18" extension leaves. Top measures
40" x 26" closed; 40" x 58" with drop leaves up; 40" x 94" with leaves up and
extension leaves in place. Height 29". ($1,550-2,000)

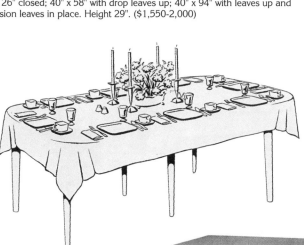

M 199 G – Console Extension Table
(1950-52) Size of top closed, 38" x 20".
Extends to 76" with three 12" leaves
inserted and top extended. Fitted with two
folding legs under top for added support
when extended. Steam-bent front boxing.
Height 29". Sketch of M 199 G fully
extended shows folding legs in position.
($1,000-1,100)

M 394 G – Service Table (1951-53) Fitted with ball-bearing caster wheels. Roomy lower shelf. Size of top, with leaves up as shown to the right, 48" x 38". With both leaves down, as shown below, 38" x 20". Height 28 ½". ($1,250-1,500)

M 786 G – Pedestal Extension Table (1952-55) Same base and butterfly construction as M 197 G but with two pedestals instead of three. Oval top measures 54" x 38" with both leaves up; with both leaves down as shown, 23" x 38". Fitted with two 12" aproned leaves, top extends to 78". ($1,550-1,800)

M 189 G – Junior Dining Extension Table (1952-55) Fitted with 18" leaf with aprons to match boxing. Top measures 36" x 54" closed; 36" x 72" open. Height 29". ($1,000-1,200)

M 789 G – Large Dining Extension Table (1953-55) Fitted with center leg and two 15" leaves that can be stored under top when not in use. Top measures 60" x 42" closed; extends to 75" and 90". Height 29". ($1,750-2,000)

M 787 G – Game Dining Table (1952-54) Size of top with both leaves down, 22" x 36"; with both drop leaves raised. 40" x 36". Top extends to 88" with four 12" leaves inserted. ($800-900)

M 788 G – Extension Game Dining Table (1953-55) Fitted with two 15" leaves. As shown at left, top measures 34" x 34" closed; with one leaf in, 34" x 49"; with both leaves (as shown below), 34" x 64". Height 29". ($900-1,000)

M 950 G – Round Extension Table (1954-55) Size of top closed (as shown) 48" in diameter. With one 14" extension leaf, top measures 62" long by 48" wide. Height 29". ($2,125-2,300)

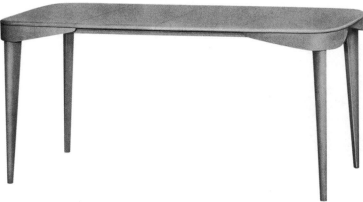

M 989 G – Drop-Leaf Extension Table (1954-55) This table has a 42" x 26 ½" top as shown above with both leaves down and no extension leaves inserted. With one drop-leaf up, the top measures 45" x 42". With both leaves up, and no extension leaves inserted the top measures 63" x 42". With two 10" leaves inserted and both drop-leaves up, the top extends to 83". ($1,200-1,450)

M 1130 G – Junior Dining Extension Table (1955-59) Contour shaped table has 14" leaf with apron to match boxing. Leaf can be stored under top when not in use. Top measures 36" x 54" closed; 36" x 68" when extended with leaf inserted. Height 29". ($700-800)

M 1133 G – Large Dining Extension Table (1955-59) Contour shaped table is fitted with center leg and has two 15" leaves with aprons to match boxing. Top measures 42" x 60" closed; 42" x 90" with two leaves inserted. Height 29". ($800-1,000)

M 952 G – Plastic Top Dining Extension Table (1955) This table is available with only Wheat, Champagne, or Platinum Plastic Top. Fitted with one 14" leaf with aprons to match boxing. Leaf can be stored under top when not in use. Top measures 34" x 48" closed; 34" x 62" when extended with leaf inserted. ($300-400)

M 1129 G – Drop-Leaf Dining Extension Table (1955-59) Butterfly supports for drop-leaves keep table top level when extended; center legs offer added rigidity at every table size. Top measures 42" x 26 ½" closed, 42" x 45" with one leaf up; 42" x 63" with both leaves up; 42" x 83" with leaves up and two 10" leaves inserted. Height 29". ($800-1,000)

M 1135 G – Oval Drop-Leaf Dining Table (1956-59) Oval shaped table measures 62" x 48" with both leaves up, as shown; with one leaf up, 62" x 32"; with both leaves down, 62" x 16". Height 29". ($800-1,000)

M 1549 G – Drop-Leaf Extension Table (1956-63) Size of top with both leaves down, 42" x 26 ½"; with both leaves up, 42" x 63"; with both leaves up and top extended with two 10" leaves inserted, 42" x 83". Height 29". ($1,200-1,350)

M 1550 G – Round Extension Table (1956) Size of top closed, 48" in diameter. Extended with 14" leaf inserted, 48" x 62". Height 29". ($2,250-2,500)

M 1556 G – 2-Pedestal Drop-Leaf Extension Table (1956-61) Size of top with both leaves down, 38" x 23"; with both leaves up, 38" x 54"; with both leaves up and two 12" leaves inserted, 38" x 78". Height 29". ($1,550-1,800)

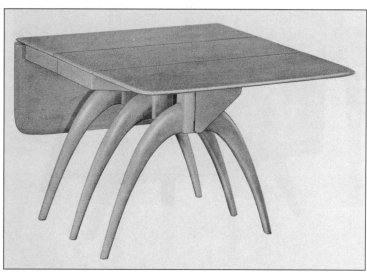

M 1557 G – 3-Pedestal Drop-Leaf Extension Table (1956-63) Size of top with both leaves down, 40" x 26"; with both leaves up, 40" x 58"; with both leaves up and two 18" leaves inserted, 40" x 94". Height 29". ($1,400-1,550)

M 1569 G – Junior Dining Extension Table (1956) Size of top 34" x 50". Top extended with 14" leaf inserted, 34" x 64". Height 29". ($650-750)

M 1558 G – Junior Dining Extension Table (1956-63) Size of top closed, 38" x 54"; top extended with 18" leaf inserted is 38" x 72". Height 29". ($700-800)

M 1567 G – Dining Extension Table (1958-59) Size of top closed, 36" x 48"; top extended with one 12", self-storing leaf inserted, 60". Height is 29". M 1567 GP same as above but has matching plastic top. ($550-650)

M 1559 G – Large Dining Extension Table (1956-61) Size of top closed, 42" x 60"; top extended with two 15" leaves inserted is 42" x 90". Height 29". ($750-850)

M 1566 G – Drop-Leaf Dining Table (1956) Size of top with both leaves down, 36" x 14"; with both leaves up, 36" x 60". Height is 29". ($650-750)

M 1568 G – Round Dining Extension Table (1958-59) Size of top 48" in diameter; top extends to 48" x 72" with two 12" leaves inserted. Height is 29". M 1568 GP same as above but has matching plastic top. ($1,750-2,000)

M 1589 G – Large Dining Extension Table (1962-63) Top: 42" x 60" – 75" – 90". H 29". Two 15" leaves have matched boxing. Fitted with Watertown steel slides. ($700-800)

M 151 A – Side Chair (1950-52) Seat measures 17" wide x 15" deep. Height of back 16". ($200-250)

M 152 A – Side Chair (1950) Seat measures 17" wide x 15" deep. Height of back 16". ($150-175)

M 153 A – Side Chair (1950) Seat measures 17" wide x 15" deep. Height of back 16". ($150-175)

M 154 A – Side Chair (1950-55) Seat measures 18" wide x 16" deep. Height of back 16 ½". ($300-400)

M 155 A – Side Chair (1950) Seat measures 18" wide x 16" deep. Height of back 15". ($300-400)

M 154 C – Arm Chair (1950-55) Seat measures 18" wide x 16" deep. Height of back 16 ½". ($375-475)

M 155 C – Arm Chair (1950) Seat measures 18" wide x 16" deep. Height of back 15". ($300-400)

M 157 A – Side Chair (1950-52) Seat measures 18" wide x 16" deep. Height of back 17". ($350-400)

M 158 A – Side Chair (1950) Seat measures 18" wide x 17" deep. Height of back 17". ($250-300)

M 157 C – Arm Chair (1950-52) Seat measures 18" wide x 16" deep. Height of back 17". ($375-475)

M 158 C – Arm Chair (1950) Seat measures 22" wide x 17" deep. Height of back 17". ($375-450)

149

M 555 A – Side Chair
(1950-55) Seat measures 18" wide x 16" deep. Height of back 16". Overall height 32". ($375-425)

M 553 A – Side Chair (1950-54) Seat measures 17" wide x 15" deep. Height of back 15". Overall height 32". ($200-250)

M 553 C – Arm Chair (1950-54) Seat measures 18" wide x 16" deep. Height of back 15". Overall height 32". ($225-275)

M 555 C – Arm Chair (1950-55) Seat measures 21" wide x 17" deep. Height of back 17". Overall height 34". ($450-500)

M 551 A – Side Chair (1952-55) Seat measures 17" wide x 16" deep. Height of back 16". ($200-225)

M 557 A – Side Chair
(1952-53) Width of seat 18 ½". Depth of seat 16". Overall height 34". ($300-350)

M 556 A – Side Chair (1952-55) Seat measures 18" wide x 16" deep. Height of back 15". Overall height 31". ($450-500)

M 557 C – Arm Chair (1952-53) Width of seat 20 ½". Depth of seat 16 ½". Overall height 35". ($375-425)

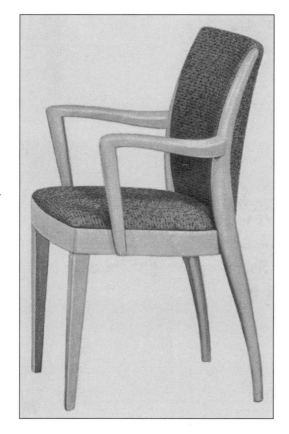

M 556 C – Arm Chair (1952-55) Seat measures 18" wide x 16" deep. Height of back 15". Overall height 31". ($475-500)

M 6107 A – Side Chair (1952) Width of seat 17". Depth 24". Height 35". ($275-325)

M 6107 C – Arm Chair (1952) Width of seat 23". Depth 24". Height 35". ($300-350)

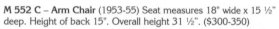

M 552 A – Side Chair (1953-55) Seat measures 18" wide x 15 ½" deep. Height of back 15". Overall height 31 ½". ($275-325)

M 552 C – Arm Chair (1953-55) Seat measures 18" wide x 15 ½" deep. Height of back 15". Overall height 31 ½". ($300-350)

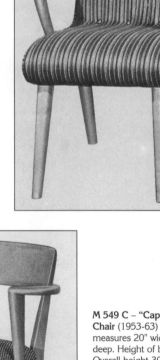

M 549 C – "Captain's" Chair (1953-63) Seat measures 20" wide x 17" deep. Height of back 14". Overall height 30". ($100-150)

M 554 A – Side Chair (1953-55) Seat measures 18" wide x 16 ½" deep. Height of back 16". Overall height 32". ($225-275)

M 953 A – Side Chair (1954-55) Seat measures 17" wide x 15" deep. Height of back 15". Overall height 32". ($225-275)

M 554 C – Arm Chair (1953-55) Seat measures 18" wide x 16 ½" deep. Height of back 16". Overall height 33 ½". ($250-300)

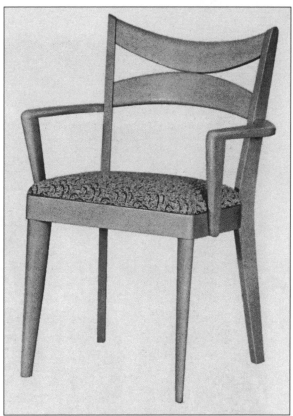

M 953 C – Arm Chair (1954-55) Seat measures 18" wide x 16" deep. Height of back 15". Overall height 32". ($350-400)

M 1132 A – Side Chair (1955-59) Seat measures 19" wide x 17" deep. Height of back 15". Foam rubber seat cushion. ($75-100)

M 1131 A – Side Chair (1955-59) Seat measures 19" wide x 17" deep. Height of back 15". ($100-125)

M 1132 C – Arm Chair (1955-59) Seat measures 19" wide x 17" deep. Height of back 15". Foam rubber seat cushion. ($100-125)

M 1134 A – Side Chair (1955-59) Seat measures 19" wide x 17" deep. Height of back 15". Cotton filled seat cushion. ($100-125)

M 1131 C – Arm Chair (1955-59) Seat measures 19" wide x 17" deep. Height of back 15". ($125-150)

M 1134 C – Arm Chair (1955-59) Seat measures 19" wide x 17" deep. Height of back 15". Cotton filled seat cushion. ($125-150)

M 1551 A – Side Chair (1956-63) Seat 18" wide x 16" deep. Back height 14 ¾". Overall height 31 ½". ($200-225)

M 1552 A – **Side Chair** (1956) Seat 19" wide x 17" deep. Back height 15". Overall height 32". ($200-225)

M 1551 C – Arm Chair (1956-63) Seat 18" wide x 16" deep. Back height 14 ¾". Overall height 31 ½". ($225-250)

M 1552 C – Arm Chair (1956) Seat 19" wide x 17" deep. Back height 15". Overall height 32". ($225-250)

M 1553 A – **Side Chair** (1956-63) Seat 18" wide x 16" deep. Back height 16 ¼". Overall height 32". ($375-425)

M **1555 A – Side Chair** (1956-59) Seat 18" wide x 16" deep. Back height 15". Overall height 32 ¼". ($350-400)

M **1553 C – Arm Chair** (1956-63) Seat 18" wide x 16" deep. Back height 16 ¼". Overall height 32". ($400-450)

M **1555 C – Arm Chair** (1956-59) Seat 18" wide x 16" deep. Back height 15". Overall height 32 ¼". ($400-450)

M **1554 A – Side Chair** (1956-63) Seat 18" wide x 16" deep. Back height 16". Overall height 32 ½". ($350-400)

M **1554 C – Arm Chair** (1956-63) Seat 18" wide x 16" deep. Back height 16". Overall height 32 ½". ($375-475)

M 1562 A – Cane Side Chair (1956) Seat 20 ½" wide x 19" deep. Back height 15". Overall height 31 ½". ($150-175)

M 1562 A RU – Cane Side Chair with Foam Rubber Seat Cushion (1956) Seat 20 ½" wide x 19" deep. Back height 13". Overall height 31 ½". ($150-175)

M 1562 C – Cane Arm Chair (1956) Seat 20 ½" wide x 19" deep. Back height 15". Overall height 31 ½". ($175-200)

M 1562 C RU – Cane Arm Chair with Foam Rubber Seat Cushion (1956) Seat 20 ½" x 19" deep. Back height 13". Overall height 31 ½". ($175-200)

157

M 1563 A – Side Chair (1956) Seat 20 ½" wide x 19" deep. Back height 14". Overall height 31 ½". ($150-175)

M 1564 A – Side Chair (1956-61) Seat 19" wide x 17" deep. Back height 16". Overall height 32". ($175-200)

M 1563 C – Arm Chair (1956) Seat 20 ½" wide x 19" deep. Back height 14". Overall height 31 ½". ($175-200)

M 1564 C – Arm Chair (1956-61) Seat 19" wide x 17" deep. Back height 16". Overall height 32". ($250-300)

M 1593 A – Side Chair (1958-59) Overall: height 34", width 19 ½", depth 20". ($150-175)

M 1594 A – Side Chair (1958-59) Overall: height 34", width 20", depth 20". ($175-200)

M 1561 A – Side Chair (1958-59) Overall: height 31 ½", width 18 ½", depth 19 ½". ($225-250)

M 1561 C – Arm Chair (1958-59) Overall: height 31 ½", width 21 ½", depth 19 ½". ($250-275)

M 1594 C – Arm Chair (1958-59) Overall: height 35", width 24 ½", depth 21". ($225-250)

159

M 176 – Corner Cabinet
(1950-55) This full size corner
cabinet is 68" high, 28" wide,
and 16" deep. Lower
compartment fitted with
adjustable shelf. ($1,250-
1,500)

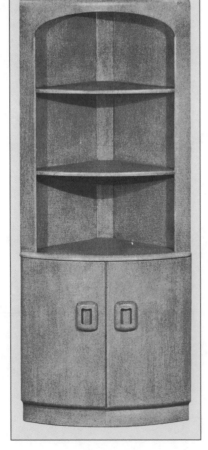

M 175 on M 190 – China (1950) The overall height of this
china is 64 ½". Server base is 34" wide, 17" deep, and 32 ½"
high. Plate glass top measures 32" wide, 14 ½" deep, and 32"
high. Both the server and the hutch have adjustable shelves.
($1,050-1,200)

M 192 – 3-Drawer Buffet (1950) Fitted with two adjustable shelves in each cabinet compartment. Top measures 48" wide by 18" deep. Height 32 ½". ($1,050-1,200)

M 334 – Utility Cabinet (1950) The base (M 334) used to form the china shown here can be used as a bedroom piece, as part of a sectional bookcase arrangement in the living room, as a separate server in the dining room, or as shown. It is 32 ½" high—the same as the curved and straight bookcase sections. The top is 34" wide and 15 ½" deep. The three drawers are extra deep. ($800-900)

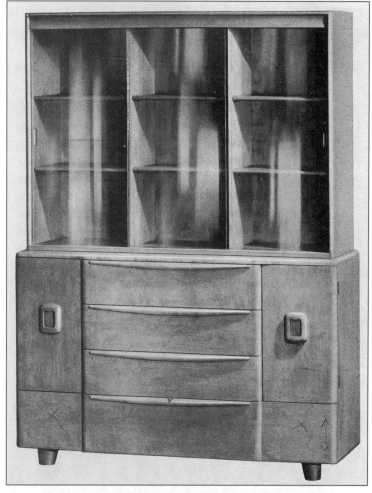

M 198 on M 193 – Credenza with Glass-Top Hutch (1950) Fitted with full length bottom drawer and adjustable shelves inside of both cabinets. Buffet top measures 54" x 18", height 34". Plate glass hutch measures 52" wide, 14" deep, and 38" high. Overall height of case 72". Top has 6 adjustable shelves. ($2,500-3,000)

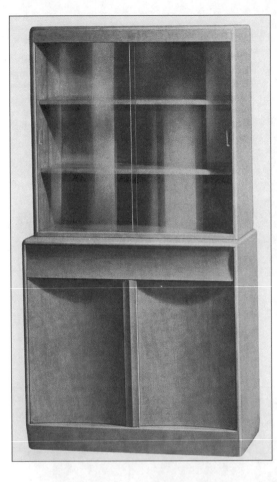

M 175 on M 194 – China (1950) The base of this china is fitted with ball-bearing, swivel wheels. The top measures 34" x 18". It stands 32 ½" high. The overall china height is 64 ½". The plate glass top is fitted with 2 adjustable shelves. The base has a full length drawer and an adjustable cabinet shelf inside. ($1,250-1,400)

M 590 – Server (1950-55) Fitted with shelf inside of cabinet doors. Top measures 34" wide and 17" deep. Height 32 ½". ($700-800)

M 198 on M 196 – Credenza with Glass-Top Hutch (1950-53) This modern utility case stands 72" overall and is equipped with ball-bearing swivel wheels. The credenza base is 54" wide and 18" deep; height 34". Plate glass top is 52" wide, 14" deep, and 38" high. The base is fitted with 3 drawers at top and a full length bottom drawer. The two base cabinets are fitted with adjustable shelves. The hutch has 6 adjustable shelves. ($2,500-3,000)

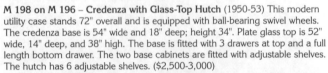

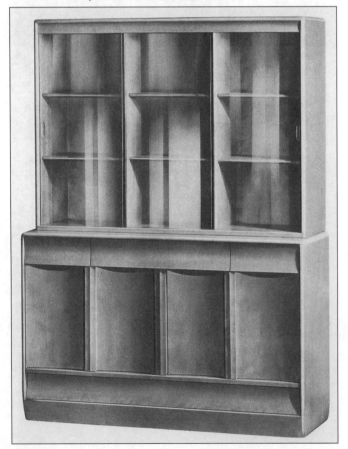

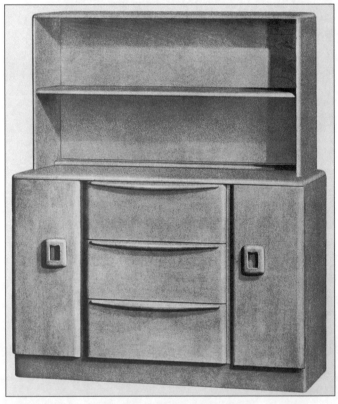

M 785 on M 592 – Open Hutch Top on Buffet (1952–54) Top of buffet measures 48" x 18". Height 32 ½". Hutch top measures 45" x 12". Height 25". Overall height of complete case 57 ½". ($1,550-1,800)

M 508 on M 592 – Glass Top Hutch on Buffet (1953–54) Glass top hutch is 44" wide, 14" deep, and 26" high. 3-Drawer buffet is fitted with two adjustable shelves in each cabinet compartment. Top measures 48" wide by 18" deep. Height 32 ½". Overall height of buffet and top is 58 ½". ($1,650-1,800)

M 527 on M 526 – China with Open Hutch (1952-53) The M 526 server base is 34" wide, 15 ½" deep, and 32 ½" high. It is fitted with two adjustable shelves inside of the cabinet doors. The M 527 open hutch is 32" wide, 12" deep, and 25" high. Overall height of china 57 ½". ($1,150-1,250)

M 999 on M 782 W – Utility Cabinet China (1952-55) The M 782 W has a drop-front desk drawer at the top. It has two adjustable shelves in the cabinet section. Base measures 48" wide, 18" deep, 34" high. China top has an adjustable shelf and measures 46" wide, 14" deep, and 26" high. Overall height of base and top 60". ($1,550-1,800)

M 509 on M 593 – Credenza with China Top (1953-54) China top measures 50" wide, 14" deep, and 39" high. Credenza is fitted with full length top drawer and adjustable shelves inside cabinets. Top measures 54" x 18". Height 34". Silver tray in top drawer. Overall height of credenza and china top is 73". ($2,200-2,500)

M 997 – Buffet with Tambour Door (1954-55) Fitted with tambour door at cabinet side. Top measures 48" wide and 19" deep. Height 31". ($1,000-1,100)

M 375 on M 996 – China (1954-55) The M 375 china top has sliding plate-glass doors. It is fitted with two adjustable shelves. Size of top 32 ½" wide, 14" deep, and 32 ½" high. The M 996 Server is fitted with adjustable shelf. Top measures 36" x 19". Height 31". Overall height of base and top 63 ½". ($1,000-1,200)

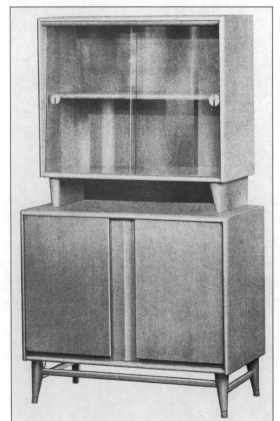

M 995 on M 996 – China (1954) Base measures 36" x 19". Height 31". China top measures 33" x 15". Height 31". Overall height 62". ($1,050-1,200)

M 909 on M 998 – Large Buffet with China Top (1954-55) China top is 50" wide x 14" deep x 38" high. It is fitted with four adjustable shelves and three drawers. Base is fitted with three drawers, an adjustable shelf in each cabinet section, and a felt-lined silver tray in the top drawer. Top measures 60" x 19". Height 31". Full piece has 6 drawers and two cabinets. Overall height of base and top 69". ($1,750-2,000)

M 1123 on M 1128 – Cane Door Cupboard (1955-59) Cupboard has two cane doors with magnetic catches, single drawer and six adjustable shelves. Top measures 57" wide, 14" deep, 39" high. Credenza has four drawers and two Tambour door compartments. Top drawer is fitted with silver tray. Each compartment has an adjustable shelf. Top measures 65" x 20 ½". Height 31 ½". Overall height of cupboard and credenza 70 ½". ($1,200-1,800)

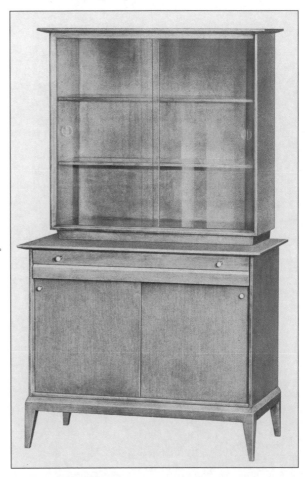

M 1125 on M 1126 – China on Server (1955-59) China top measures 37" wide, 14" deep, 33" high. Has two sliding plate-glass doors and two adjustable shelves. Server top measures 39" x 20 ½". Height 31 ½". Fitted with full-length drawer. Cabinet has two sliding doors and an adjustable shelf. Overall height of server and china 64 ½". ($1,000-1,200)

M 1124 on M 1127 – Open Hutch Buffet (1955-56) Hutch top measures 46" wide x 13" deep, 31 ½" high. Fitted with drawer. Buffet top measures 50" x 20 ½". Height 31 ½". Fitted with two drawers. Cabinet has sliding doors and two adjustable shelves. Overall height of hutch and buffet is 63". ($1,200-1,500)

M 1545 on M 1541 – Crown Glass China on Server (1956) China top has Crown Glass door panels. It is fitted with two adjustable shelves. Top measures 34" wide, 14" deep, 31" high. Server base is fitted with full-length drawer. Cabinet has shelf. Top measures 36" x 17". Height 32". Overall height of china and server is 63". ($1,750-2,000)

M 1547 on M 1543 – Large Crown Glass China on Credenza (1956-63) China top has three Crown Glass doors. Fitted with two adjustable shelves. Top measures 56" wide, 14 ¾" deep, 35" high. Buffet is fitted with four drawers and two compartments. Top drawer is for silver. Adjustable shelf in each of the end compartments. Top measures 60" x 18". Height 32". Overall height of china and buffet is 67". ($3,500-3,900)

M 1548 on M 1541 – China on Server (1956-61) China top has sliding plate glass doors. It is fitted with an adjustable shelf. Top measures 34" wide, 14" deep, 26" high. Server base is fitted with full-length drawer. Cabinet has shelf. Top measures 36" x 17". Height 32". Overall height of china and server is 58". ($1,150-1,400)

M 1546 on M 1542 – China on Tambour Buffet (1956-63) China top has two sliding plate glass doors with an adjustable shelf. Top is 45 ½" wide, 14" deep, 26" high. Buffet is fitted with three drawers and has tambour cabinet with adjustable shelf. Buffet top is 50" x 18". Height is 32". Overall height of china and buffet is 58". ($1,550-1,800)

M 1122 on M 1127 – China (1957-59) China top has sliding plate glass door panels. Fitted with two drawers, adjustable plate glass shelf and glass top. Back panel is white Plastone (plasticized) hardboard. Top measures 44" wide, 13 ½" deep, 34" high. Buffet measures 50" wide, 20 ½" deep, 31 ½" high. Fitted with silver drawer lined with non-tarnish cloth, and a utility drawer. Cabinet has sliding doors and two adjustable shelves. Overall height of china top and buffet is 65 ½". ($1,050-1,300)

M 1547 on M 1544 – Large Crown Glass China on Credenza (1957-61)
China top has three Crown Glass doors. Fitted with two adjustable shelves. Top measures 56" wide, 14 ¾" deep, 35" high. Top left drawer of credenza has silver compartments lined with non-tarnishing cloth. Drawer at top right has center partition. Single door compartment at lower left has adjustable shelf. Two door compartment has two tray-drawers. Credenza has four caster wheels. Top measures 60" x 18". Height 32". Overall height of china and credenza is 67". ($3,500-3,800)

M 1596 on M 1542 – Glass Door Hutch Top on Tambour Buffet (1958-59) Hutch top has glass doors; center section has two adjustable shelves. Top measures 45 ½" wide, 14 ¼" deep, 35" high. Buffet is fitted with three drawers and has tambour cabinet with adjustable shelf. Buffet is 50" x 18". Height is 32". Overall height of hutch and buffet is 67". ($1,500-1,700)

M 1546 on M 1592 – China (1957-58) China top has sliding plate glass doors. Fitted with an adjustable shelf. Top measures 45 ½" wide, 14" deep, 26" high. Buffet is fitted with four drawers; top drawer is lined and partitioned for silver. Tambour cabinet has an adjustable shelf. Buffet measures 50" wide, 18" deep, 32" high. Overall height of china top and buffet is 58". ($1,550-1,800)

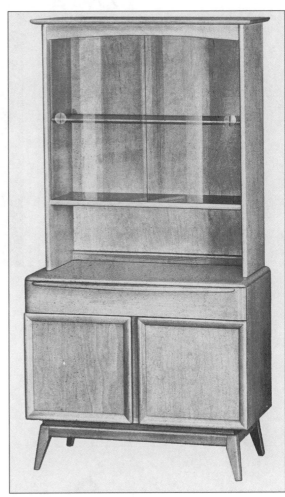

M 1598 on M 1597 – Glass Door Hutch on Server (1962-63) Glass door hutch measurements: width 36", depth 13 ½", height 39". Two sliding plate glass doors. One long adjustable shelf. Server measurements: width 36", depth 18", height 30". Full-length drawer has four partitions lined with non-tarnishing cloth for silver. Two door storage compartment has adjustable shelf. ($1,050-1,300)

Bedrooms

Nearly all of Heywood-Wakefield's Modern furniture for the bedroom was designed in matched suites or ensembles, many attributed to the various designers who lent their talent to the company. Bearing romantic names such as Airflow, Cameo, Crescendo, Rio, Kohinoor, and Sculptura, the bedroom suites truly showcase Heywood-Wakefield's fondness for rounded edges and soft curves—design elements surely appropriate for this room of the home.

Given the suite nature of Heywood's bedroom furniture, this portion of the book has been further broken down accordingly. The 1930s and 1940s pictures are organized by lines first, then chronologically *within* lines. Those few pieces not identified as belonging to a particular line or suite have been simply placed in their appropriate chronological location. The 1950s section begins with a pictorial overview of bedroom suites from that era, followed by individual images organized functionally (i.e., beds, dressers, vanities, etc.) and then by line.

If not otherwise identified, the quoted material regarding bedroom suites is taken from Heywood-Wakefield catalogs and other literature.

1930s and 1940s – The Streamline Years

Zephyr

This early bedroom grouping was characterized by medallion type drawer pulls, sleek rounded drawer fronts, and a reeded effect on some pieces. The pieces are shown here in Bleached finish and were available in Amber as well.

C 3158 – Night Stand (1936-37) Size of top 10 ½" x 15". Bottom depth 18". Height 23 ½". *Available* in Amber, Bleached, combination of Amber and Bleached. ($250-325)

C 3150 – Bed (1936-37) Available in 3' 3" and 4' 6" sizes. *Available* in Amber or Bleached. ($350-400)

C 3151 – 3 Drawer Dresser (1936-37) Size of top 39 ½" x 19". Height 33 ½". *Available* in Amber, Bleached, combination of Amber and Bleached. ($650-800)

C 3153 – Oblong Mirror (1936-37) Size 30" x 22". *Available* in Amber or Bleached. ($200-250)

C 3156 – Dressing Table (1936-37) Size of top 34" x 17". Height 30". *Available* in Amber, Bleached, combination of Amber and Bleached. ($650-750)

C 3135 – Round Mirror (1936-37) Size 30" in diameter. *Available* in Amber or Bleached. ($225-250)

C 3157 – Bench (1936-37) Size of top 24" x 15". Height 17". *Available* in Amber or Bleached. ($250-300)

C 3158 – Night Stand (1936-37) Size of top 10 ½" x 15". Bottom depth 18". Height 23 ½". *Available* in Amber, Bleached, combination of Amber and Bleached. ($250-325)

C 3150 – Bed (1936-37) Available in 3' 3" and 4' 6" sizes. *Available* in Amber or Bleached. ($350-400)

C 3152 – 4 Drawer Chest (1936-37) Size of top 30 ½" x 19". Height 43". *Available* in Amber, Bleached, combination of Amber and Bleached. ($700-850)

C 3154 – Vanity (1936-37) Size of top 42" x 18". Height 25 ½". *Available* in Amber, Bleached, combination of Amber and Bleached. ($650-800)

C 3135 – Round Mirror (1936-37) Size 30" in diameter. *Available* in Amber or Bleached. ($225-250)

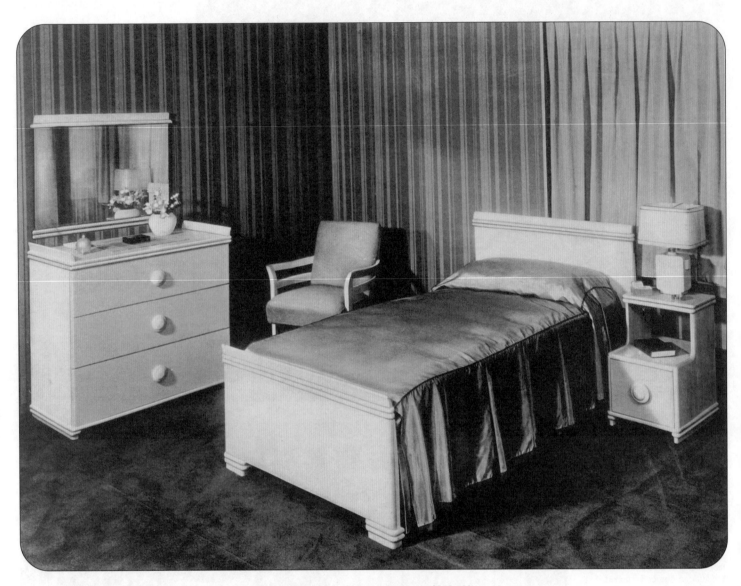

C 3150 – Bed (1936-37) Available in 3' 3" and 4' 6" sizes. *Available* in Amber or Bleached. ($350-400)

C 3151 – 3 Drawer Dresser (1936-37) Size of top 39 ½" x 19". Height 33 ½". *Available* in Amber, Bleached, combination of Amber and Bleached. ($650-800)

C 3153 X – Mirror (1937) Size 34" x 22". *Available* in Amber or Bleached. ($175-225)

C 3158 – Night Stand (1936-37) Size of top 10 ½" x 15". Bottom depth 18". Height 23 ½". *Available* in Amber, Bleached, combination of Amber and Bleached. ($250-325)

C 3325 C – Occasional Chair (1937-40) Seat 20" x 18 ½". Height of back 18 ½".. *Available* in Wheat, Champagne, Amber, Bleached, or Modern Walnut. ($850-950)

Penthouse

Featuring "clean, simple lines…," the Penthouse suite could be ordered with an interesting finish combination using both Amber and Bleached. See the Appendix (pages 237-238) for more information on this unusual treatment.

C 3168 – Night Stand (1936-37) Size of top 14" x 13". Height 24 ¾". *Available* in Amber, Bleached, combination of Amber and Bleached. ($225-275)

C 3160 – Bed (1936-37) Available in 3' 3" and 4' 6" sizes. *Available* in Amber or Bleached. ($300-400)

C 3162 – 5 Drawer Chest (1936-37) Size of top 31 ½" x 19". Height 41 ½". *Available* in Amber, Bleached, combination of Amber and Bleached. ($650-800)

C 3135 – Round Mirror (1936-37) Size 30" in diameter. *Available* in Amber or Bleached. ($225-250)

C 3166 – Dressing Table (1936-37) Size of top 34" x 17". Height 30". *Available* in Amber, Bleached, combination of Amber and Bleached. ($650-800)

C 3167 – Bench (1936-37) Size of top 23" x 15". Height 19". *Available* in Amber or Bleached. ($175-250)

C 3161 – 4 Drawer Dresser (1936-37) Size of top 40" x 19". Height 34". *Available* in Amber, Bleached, combination of Amber and Bleached. ($650-800)

C 3163 – Oblong Mirror (1936-37) Size 22" x 34". *Available* in Amber or Bleached. ($250-300)

C 2787 C – Arm Chair (1936-40) Width of seat 24". Depth of seat 20". Height of back 15". *Available* in Wheat, Champagne, Amber, Bleached, and Modern Walnut. ($750-900)

C 3167 – Bench (1936-37) Size of top 23" x 15". Height 19". *Available* in Amber or Bleached. ($175-250)

C 3164 – Vanity (1936-37) Size of top 44" x 18". Height 30 ½". *Available* in Amber, Bleached, combination of Amber and Bleached. ($1,050-1,200)

C 3135 – Round Mirror (1936-37) Size 30" in diameter. *Available* in Amber or Bleached. ($225-275)

This grouping had no specific line name, but was shown in the *Streamline Maple* catalog of 1936.

C 2909 – Bed (1936-37) Available in 3' 3" and 4' 6" sizes. *Available* in Amber or Bleached. ($375-475)

C 2902 – 4 Drawer Chest (1936-37) Top 32" x 19". Height 43". *Available* in Amber, Bleached, combination of Amber and Bleached. ($750-900)

C 2908 – Night Stand (1936-37) Top 14" x 13". Height 25 ½". *Available* in Amber, Bleached, combination of Amber and Bleached. ($300-400)

C 2901 – 3 Drawer Dresser (1936-37) Top 40" x 19". Height 43". *Available* in Amber, Bleached, combination of Amber or Bleached. ($750-900)

C 2903 – Mirror (1936-37) Size 19" x 29". *Available* in Amber or Bleached. ($150-250)

C 2920 C – Arm Chair (1936-37) Reversible spring filled back and seat cushions. Width of seat 22". Depth of seat 23". Height of back 18". *Available* in Amber or Bleached. ($1,050-1,250)

C 2910 – Center Cabinet (1936-37) May be used in bedroom groupings or as the center section of a three piece buffet. Size of top 32" x 19". Height 34". *Available* in Amber, Bleached, combination of Amber and Bleached. ($900-1,000)

C 2907 – Bench (1936-37) Size of top 21" x 13". Height 17". *Available* in Amber or Bleached. ($200-250)

C 2906 – Dressing Table (1936-37) Top 34" x 17". Height 30". *Available* in Amber, Bleached, combination of Amber and Bleached. ($650-750)

C 2903 – Mirror (1936-37) Size 19" x 29". *Available* in Amber or Bleached. ($150-250)

C 2931 – 5 Drawer Chest (1936-37) Size of top 40" x 19". Height 34". *Available* in Amber, Bleached, combination of Amber and Bleached. ($1,000-1,150)

C 2900 – Bed (1936-37) Available in 3' 3" or 4' 6" sizes. *Available* in Amber or Bleached. ($300-400)

C 2908 – Night Stand (1936-37) Top 14" x 13". Height 25 ½". *Available* in Amber, Bleached, combination of Amber and Bleached. ($300-400)

C 2910 – Center Cabinet (1936-37) May be used in bedroom groupings or as the center section of a three piece buffet. Size of top 32" x 19". Height 34". *Available* in Amber, Bleached, combination of Amber and Bleached. ($900-1,000)

C 2913 – Closed Cabinet (1936-37) This piece may be used on the C 2917 Server to form a closed dining hutch or on the C 2910 to form a chest on chest for bedroom use. Size 31" x 14". Height 17". *Available* in Amber or Bleached. ($375-475)

173

C 2907 – Bench (1936-37) Size of top 21" x 13". Height 17". *Available* in Amber or Bleached. ($200-250)

C 2904 – Vanity (1936-37) Overall length 42". Depth 17". Height 30 ¾". *Available* in Amber, Bleached, combination of Amber and Bleached. ($900-1,000)

C 2905 – Mirror (1936-37) Size 22" x 34". *Available* in Amber or Bleached. ($225-300)

Airflow

Designed by Leo Jiranek, the Airflow group was a mainstay of the early bedroom suites and featured a double reeded design motif on drawer pulls, beds, etc. Rounded fronts gave the suite an air of elegance. As noted in the catalog: "Rounded or 'swell-fronts' are employed in the 'Airflow' design. These graceful bends of *solid wood* are one of the most difficult achievements in all furniture making … possible only with special, expensive machinery which Heywood-Wakefield first developed more than 60 years ago."

Bed options included the C 3360 with cane panels (see next page). The company recommended that this bed be ordered in the Wheat finish, as it "enhances the natural beauty of the woven cane."

C 3330 – Bed (1937-39) Available in 3' 3" and 4' 6" sizes. *Available* in Wheat, Champagne, Amber, or Bleached. ($500-600)

C 3338 – Night Stand (1937-39) Size of top 14" x 14". Height 25 ½". *Available* in Wheat, Champagne, Amber, or Bleached. ($375-450)

C 3332 – 5-Drawer Chest (1937-39) Size of top 32" x 19". Height 46". *Available* in Wheat, Champagne, Amber, or Bleached. ($1,250-1,450)

C 3334 – Vanity (1937-39) Top 42" x 19". Height 30". *Available* in Wheat, Champagne, Amber, or Bleached. ($1,250-1,450)

C 3335 – Mirror (1937-39) Size 36" in diameter. *Available* in Wheat, Champagne, Amber, or Bleached. ($200-300)

C 3340 – Vanity with Large Mirror (1937-39) Size of top 52" x 18". Height 22". Size of mirror 48" in diameter. Overall height of vanity with mirror attached 60 ½". *Available* in Wheat, Champagne, Amber, or Bleached. ($1,500-1,800)

C 3337 – Bench (1937-38) Size of top 18" in diameter. Height 16". *Available* in Wheat, Amber, or Bleached. ($250-300)

C 2787 C – Arm Chair (1936-40) Width of seat 24". Depth of seat 20". Height of back 15". *Available* in Wheat, Champagne, Amber, Bleached, and Modern Walnut. ($750-900)

C 3338 – Night Stand (1937-39) Size of top 14" x 14". Height 25 ½". *Available* in Wheat, Champagne, Amber, or Bleached. ($375-450)

C 3330 – Bed (1937-39) Available in 3' 3" and 4' 6" sizes. *Available* in Wheat, Champagne, Amber, or Bleached. ($500-600)

C 3325 C – Occasional Chair (1937-40) Seat 20" x 18 ½". Height of back 18 ½".. *Available* in Wheat, Champagne, Amber, Bleached, or Modern Walnut. ($850-950)

C 3331 – 4-Drawer Dresser (1937-39) Size of top 42" x 20". Height 34". *Available* in Wheat, Champagne, Amber, or Bleached. ($1,150-1,350)

C 3333 – Mirror (1937-39) Size 22" x 34". *Available* in Wheat, Champagne, Amber, or Bleached. ($250-350)

C 3360 – Cane Panel Bed (1938) Available in 3' 3" and 4' 6" sizes. *Available* in Wheat Finish. ($375-475)

C 3331 – 4-Drawer Dresser (1937-39) Size of top 42" x 20". Height 34". *Available* in Wheat, Champagne, Amber, or Bleached. ($1,150-1,250)

C 3333 – Mirror (1937-39) Size 22" x 34". *Available* in Wheat, Champagne, Amber, or Bleached. ($250-350)

C 3338 – Night Stand (1937-39) Size of top 14" x 14". Height 25 ½". *Available* in Wheat, Champagne, Amber, or Bleached. ($375-450)

C 3325 C – Occasional Chair (1937-40) Seat 20" x 18 ½". Height of back 18 ½".. *Available* in Wheat, Champagne, Amber, Bleached, or Modern Walnut. ($850-950)

Shown in the 1937 and 1938 catalogs, this bedroom group was not given a specific name. Design elements include a double reeded motif as in the Airflow group—but placed horizontally on the pieces, rather than vertically as in Airflow.

C 3300 – Bed (1937-38) Available in 3' 3" or 4' 6" sizes. *Available* in Wheat, Amber, or Bleached. ($375-475)

C 3302 – 4-Drawer Chest (1937-38) Top 32" x 19". Height 43". *Available* in Wheat, Amber, or Bleached. ($850-1,000)

C 3308 – Night Stand (1937-38) Top 14" x 13". Height 25 ½". *Available* in Wheat, Amber, or Bleached. ($250-300)

C 3309 – Bed (1937-38) Available in 3' 3" or 4' 6" sizes. *Available* in Wheat, Amber, or Bleached. ($375-475)

C 3301 – 3-Drawer Dresser (1937-38) Top 40" x 19". Height 34". *Available* in Wheat, Amber, or Bleached. ($800-950)

C 3303 – Mirror (1937-38) Glass size 20" x 30". *Available* in Wheat, Amber, or Bleached. ($225-275)

C 3306 – Dressing Table (1937-38) Top 38" x 17". Height 30". *Available* in Wheat, Amber, or Bleached. ($800-1,000)

C 3324 AX – Side Chair (1937-38) Seat 16" x 14". Height of back 16 ½". *Available* in Wheat, Amber, Bleached, or Modern Walnut. ($550-650)

C 3304 – Vanity (1937-38) Overall length 42". Depth 17". Height 30 ¾". *Available* in Wheat, Amber, or Bleached. ($800-1,000)

C 3307 – Bench (1937-38) Size of top 21" x 13". Height 17". *Available* in Wheat, Amber, or Bleached. ($200-250)

C 3305 – Mirror (1937-38) Size 22" x 34". *Available* in Wheat, Amber, or Bleached. ($200-250)

Swedish Modern

A bedroom set characterized by rounded breakfronts on all major pieces and natural fiber on the drawer pulls and headboards. The 1939 catalog notes that this "conservative, well-proportioned design" was popular for hotel use as well as home use.

C 3370 – Bed (1938) Available in 3' 3" or 4' 6" sizes. *Available* in Wheat, Amber, or Bleached. ($450-550)

C 3371-75 – Dresser with Attached Round Mirror (1938) Size of dresser top 42" x 20". Height 33". Size of round mirror 30" in diameter. *Available* in Wheat, Amber, or Bleached. ($1,050-1,150)

C 3378 – Night Stand (1938) Fitted with drop-door on lower compartment. Size of top 14" x 13". Height 26". *Available* in Wheat, Amber, or Bleached. ($250-300)

C 3325 C – Occasional Chair (1937-40) Seat 20" x 18 ½". Height of back 18 ½".. *Available* in Wheat, Champagne, Amber, Bleached, or Modern Walnut. ($850-950)

C 3370 – Bed (1938) Available in 3' 3" or 4' 6" sizes. *Available* in Wheat, Amber, or Bleached. ($450-550)

C 3372 – 4-Drawer Chest (1938) Top drawer divided into three sections; second drawer into two compartments. Size of top 32" x 19". Height 45 ½". *Available* in Wheat, Amber, or Bleached. ($1,200-1,350)

C 3374 – Vanity (1938) Size of top 42" x 18". Height 26". *Available* in Wheat, Amber, or Bleached. ($900-1,000)

C 3373 – Mirror (1938) Size 24" x 30". *Available* in Wheat, Amber, or Bleached. ($300-400)

C 3377 – Bench (1938) Size of top 22" x 13". Height 16". *Available* in Wheat, Amber, or Bleached. ($200-250)

C 3378 – Night Stand (1938) Fitted with drop-door on lower compartment. Size of top 14" x 13". Height 26". *Available* in Wheat, Amber, or Bleached. ($250-300)

C 3376-80 – Vanity with Attached Mirror (1938) Fitted with sliding tray in upper right hand drawer. Size of top 52" x 18". Height 22". Mirror alone is 40" high by 38" wide. Overall height of Vanity with attached Mirror is 62". *Available* in Wheat, Amber, or Bleached. ($1,050-1,200)

C 3379 – Vanity Seat (1938-39) Size of top 18" in diameter. Height 15". *Available* in Wheat, Champagne, Amber, or Bleached. ($300-400)

C 2787 C – Arm Chair (1936-40) Width of seat 24". Depth of seat 20". Height of back 15". *Available* in Wheat, Champagne, Amber, Bleached, and Modern Walnut. ($750-900)

Crescendo

Designed by Count Alexis de Sakhnoffsky, the "simple and stately" Crescendo bedroom suite featured "gracefully flowing lines and rounded fronts."

C 3550 – Bed (1939-40) Available in 3' 3" and 4' 6" sizes. *Available* in Wheat, Champagne, Amber, or Bleached. ($375-475)

C 3551-55 – Dresser with Mirror Attached (1939-40) Size of top 42" x 20". Height 33 ½". Size of mirror 26" x 40". Overall height 61". *Available* in Wheat, Champagne, Amber, or Bleached. ($1,000-1,150)

C 3559 – Blanket Bench (1939) Fitted with large drawer. Size of top 44" x 14". Height 17". *Available* in Wheat, Champagne, Amber, or Bleached. ($1,000-1,200)

C 3558 – Night Stand (1939-40) Size of top 14" x 14". Height 25". *Available* in Wheat, Champagne, Amber, or Bleached. ($500-650)

C 3554 – Vanity (1939-40) Size of top 54" x 18". Height of base 22". Overall height 58 ½". *Available* in Wheat, Champagne, Amber, or Bleached. ($1,250-1,500)

C 3557 – Vanity Seat (1939-40) Fitted with revolving top. Seat 20" in diameter. Height 17". *Available* in Wheat, Champagne, Amber, or Bleached. ($300-400)

C 2787 C – Arm Chair (1936-40) Width of seat 24". Depth of seat 20". Height of back 15". *Available* in Wheat, Champagne, Amber, Bleached, or Modern Walnut. ($750-900)

C 3539 W – Vanity Base or Kneehole Desk (1939-40) Size of top 48" x 21". Height 30". Fully finished including rear. *Available* in Wheat, Champagne, Amber, or Bleached. ($1,850-2,150)

C 3553 – Mirror (1939-40) Size 26" x 40". *Available* in Wheat, Champagne, Amber, or Bleached. ($250-350)

C 3535 A – Side Chair (1939-43) Seat 16" x 16 ½". Height of back 17". *Available* in Wheat, Champagne, Amber, or Bleached. ($375-475)

C 3552 – 5-Drawer Chest (1939-40) Top 32" x 19". Height 48". *Available* in Wheat, Champagne, Amber, or Bleached. ($1,250-1,500)

C 3550 – Bed (1939-40) Available in 3' 3" and 4' 6" sizes. *Available* in Wheat, Champagne, Amber, or Bleached. ($375-475)

C 3551-555 – Dresser with Attached Mirror (1940) Size of dresser top 42" x 20". Height 33". Mirror size 26"x 40". Overall height complete is 61. *Available* in Wheat, Champagne, Walnut. ($1,000-1,150)

C 3558 – Night Stand (1939-40) Size of top 14" x 14". Height 25". *Available* in Wheat, Champagne, Amber, or Bleached. ($500-650)

C 3739 – Blanket Bench (1940-42) Size of upholstered, hinged top 40" x 14". Height 17 ½". *Available* in Wheat, Champagne, Amber, or Bleached. ($1,000-1,200)

Appearing quite similar to the pieces shown on pages 177-178, this group was shown in the 1939 catalog but given no specific line name. It was a lower priced set of bedroom furniture, designed to appeal to "young and prospective" homemakers seeking a well-styled yet economical line of Modern furniture.

C 3570 – Bed (1939) Available in 3' 3" and 4' 6" sizes. *Available* in Wheat, Champagne, Amber, or Bleached. ($375-425)

C 3578 – Night Stand (1939) Size of top 13" x 14". Height 25 ½". *Available* in Wheat, Champagne, Amber, or Bleached. ($300-350)

C 3572 – 4-Drawer Chest (1939) Size of top 32" x 19". Height 43". *Available* in Wheat, Champagne, Amber, or Bleached. ($1,050-1,150)

C 3574 – Vanity (1939) Top 42" x 18". Height 25". *Available* in Wheat, Champagne, Amber, or Bleached. ($800-900)

C 3573 – Mirror (1939) Glass size 34" x 18". *Available* in Wheat, Champagne, Amber, or Bleached. ($200-250)

C 3577 – Bench (1939) Size of top 13" x 21". Height 17". *Available* in Wheat, Champagne, Amber, or Bleached. ($175-225)

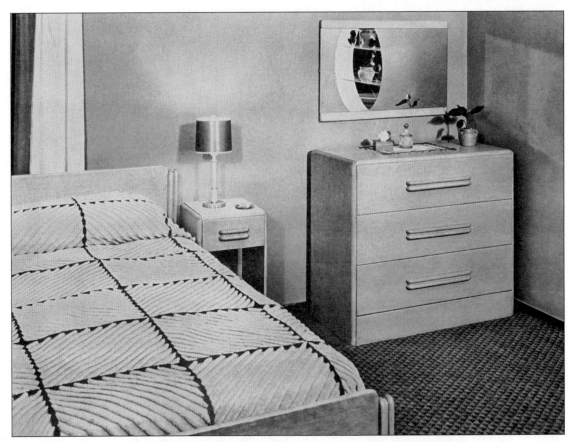

C 3570 – Bed (1939) Available in 3' 3" and 4' 6" sizes. *Available* in Wheat, Champagne, Amber, or Bleached. ($375-425)

C 3578 – Night Stand (1939) Size of top 13" x 14". Height 25 ½". *Available* in Wheat, Champagne, Amber, or Bleached. ($300-350)

C 3571 – 3-Drawer Dresser (1939) Size of top 19" x 40". Height 34". *Available* in Wheat, Champagne, Amber, or Bleached. ($850-950)

C 3573 – Mirror (1939) Glass size 34" x 18". *Available* in Wheat, Champagne, Amber, or Bleached. ($200-250)

Skyliner

Produced for two years, the Skyliner bedroom suite was described by the company as having "rounded edges, sleek drawer pulls, and simple lines of good Modern." Note the unusually designed night stand.

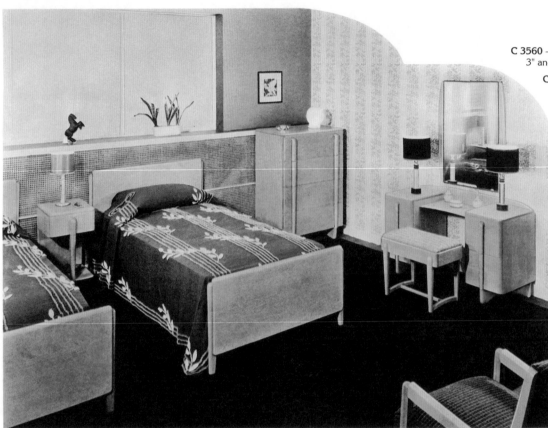

C 3560 – Bed (1939-40) Available in 3' 3" and 4' 6" sizes. ($375-425)

C 3568 – Night Stand (1939-40) Size of top 14" x 14". Height 25 ½". Fitted with one drawer. ($650-750)

C 3562 – 4-Drawer Chest (1939-40) Size of top 32" x 19". Height 45". ($1,250-1,500)

C 3564 – Vanity (1939-40) Overall size of top 45" x 18". Height 25 ½". ($1,050-1,200)

C 3563 – Hanging Mirror (1939-40) Size of glass 34" x 22". ($250-350)

C 3567 – Vanity Bench (1939-40) Size of top 21" x 13". Height 17". ($300-400)

C 3560 – Bed (1939-40) Available in 3' 3" and 4' 6" sizes. ($375-425)

C 3561 – 3-Drawer Dresser Base (1939-40) Size of top 42" x 19". Height 33 ½". ($1,250-1,500)

C 3563 – Hanging Mirror (1939-40) Size of glass 34" x 22". ($250-350)

C 3561-725 – Dresser with Attached Mirror (1939-40) This piece is not shown but it is the same Dresser Base as above with 30" round mirror attached. ($1,250-1,500)

C 3568 – Night Stand (1939-40) Size of top 14" x 14". Height 25 ½". Fitted with one drawer. ($650-750)

C 3325 C – Occasional Chair (1937-40) Seat 20" x 18 ½". Height of back 18 ½". ($850-950)

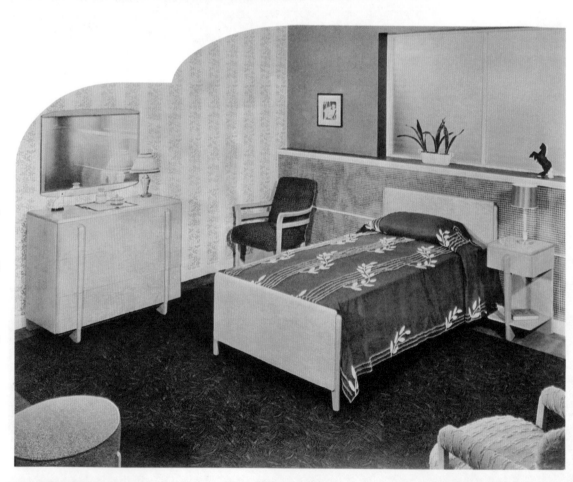

Textured Modern

As noted on page 31, these "Textured Modern" pieces may have been manufactured for a brief time only or perhaps not at all. They were shown only in a small 1939 brochure with no accompanying price list or other documentation.

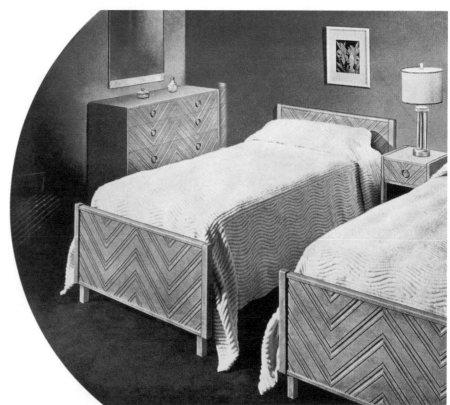

C 3500 – Bed (1939) Available in twin or full sizes. ($300-400)

C 3501 – Dresser Base (1939) 4-drawer type with a 41" x 18" top. ($400-500)

C 3503 – Mirror (1939) Measures 24" x 36". ($150-250)

C 3504 – Vanity Base (1939) The 4-drawer vanity base has a 46" x 18" top. The attached mirror is 32" wide and 26" high. ($500-600)

C 3507 – Vanity Bench (1939) The 14" x 17 ½" slip seat on the bench affords a bright color "spot." ($150-200)

This unidentified bedroom set was shown in the same 1939 brochure as the Textured Modern group. It is possible that it, too, was never actually produced.

C 3390 – Bed (1939) Available in twin or full sizes. ($300-400)

C 3392 – 4-Drawer Chest (1939) Top measures 32" x 19". ($650-750)

Plaza

More "sleek, rounded breakfronts" are found on this 1940 set designed by Leo Jiranek.

C 3730 – Bed (1940) Available in 3' 3" and 4' 6" sizes. ($375-475)

C 3731-733 – Dresser with Attached Mirror (1940) Size of top 42" x 20". Height 35". Mirror 26" x 32". ($1,000-1,150)

C 3731 – Dresser Base (1940) This is the separate base without the mirror attached. ($1,150-1,300)

C 3733 – Hanging Mirror (1940) This is the separate, hanging mirror without attachment fixtures. ($150-175)

C 3738 – Night Stand (1940) Size of top 14" square. Height 25 ½". ($375-425)

C 3732 – 5-Drawer Chest (1940)
Size of top 33" x 20". Height 48".
($1,150-1,300)

C 3736 – Vanity Desk (1940) This is
a 5-Drawer base. Top 44" x 18".
Height 30". ($1,250-1,500)

C 3735 – Hanging Mirror (1940-42)
Glass size 36" in diameter. ($200-250)

C 3596 A – Side Chair (1940-44)
Seat 16" x 16". Height of back 16".
($200-225)

C 3734 – Vanity (1940) Size of top 52" x 18".
Height of base 22". Overall height 60 ¼".
Mirror 48" in diameter. ($1,050-1,200)

C 3737 – Vanity Seat (1940) Fitted with
revolving top. Seat 19" in diameter. Height 16".
($200-250)

Challenger

Featuring large, centrally placed drawer pulls, this was another economically priced bedroom group. It was described for the company sales force as "an excellent 'traffic builder' [that] brings in the young homemakers."

C 3740 – Bed (1940) Available in 3' 3" and 4' 6" sizes. ($300-400)

C 3741 – 3-Drawer Dresser Base (1940) Size of top 40" x 19". Height 34". ($500-650)

C 3743 – Hanging Mirror (1940) Size of glass 30" x 22". ($200-250)

C 3741-725 – Dresser with Attached Mirror (1940) This piece is not shown but it is the same dresser base as above with 30" round mirror attached. ($650-800)

C 3748 – Night Stand (1940) Size of top 14" x 13". Height 25 ½". ($200-250)

C 3765 C – Arm Chair (1940-42) Seat 22" x 20". Height of back 16". ($750-900)

C 3744 – Vanity Base (1940) Size of top 42" x 18". Height 25". This is a four-drawer type vanity. ($300-400)

C 3743 – Hanging Mirror (1940) Size of glass 30" x 22". ($200-250)

C 3747 – Vanity Bench (1940) Size of seat 22" x 16". Height 16 ½". ($150-175)

C 3742 – 4-Drawer Chest (1940) Size of top 32" x 19". Height 43". ($550-700)

Cameo

Spanning a three-year period of production, the Cameo bedroom was designed as "a modern interpretation of the blockfront design used in Colonial days, but with softened, rounded edges to give added sleekness." Cameo pieces came with drawer pulls made of either Tenite (a "translucent plastic with a slightly pinkish cast") or wood. The company advised that Tenite pulls looked best with a Champagne finish, while wood pulls looked best with Wheat. Tenite pulls are shown in the first three pictures here; wood pulls can be seen in the last picture (page 190).

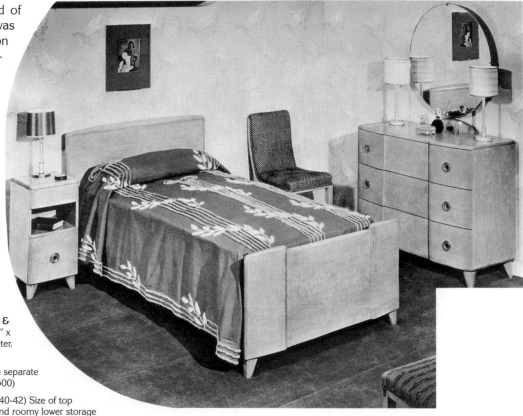

C 3720 – Bed (1940-42) Available in 3' 3" and 4' 6" sizes. ($650-750)

C 3721-725 – Dresser with Attached Mirror & Plastic Pulls (1940-42) Size of dresser top 42" x 20". Height 34". Attached mirror 30" in diameter. Overall height 67". ($500-600)

C 3721 – Dresser Base (1940-42) This is the separate dresser base without mirror attached. ($400-500)

C 3728 – Night Stand with Plastic Pulls (1940-42) Size of top 13" x 13". Height 26". Has small top drawer and roomy lower storage drawer. Open center compartment conveniently located. ($200-250)

C 3535 A – Side Chair (1939-43) Seat 16 ½" x 16 ½". Height of back 17". ($375-475)

C 3724 – Vanity Base with Plastic Pulls (1940-42) Size of top 49" x 18". Height of base 23". Overall height 59". Mirror 40" in diameter. ($375-575)

C 3727 – Vanity Seat (1940-42) The kapok filled top measures 23" x 17". Height 17". ($200-250)

C 3722 – 4-Drawer Chest with Plastic Pulls (1940-42) Size of top 32" x 19". Height 46". ($750-850)

C 3726 – Vanity Base with Plastic Pulls (1940-42) May be used as a kneehole desk because it is finished in rear as well as in front. This is a 5-drawer type. Size of top 44" x 18". Height 30". ($650-750)

C 3723 – Hanging Mirror (1940-42) Glass size 24" x 30". ($200-250)

C 3701 A – Side Chair (1940) Seat 16" x 15". Height of back 16". ($175-200)

C 3726 X – Vanity Base with Wood Pulls (1941-42) May be used as kneehole desk because it is finished in rear as well as front. This is a 5-drawer type. Size of top 44" x 18". Height 30". ($700-800)

C 3723 – Hanging Mirror (1940-42) Glass size 24" x 30". ($200-250)

C 3595 A – Side Chair (1940-44) Seat 16" x 17". Height of back 16". ($150-200)

C 3722 X – 4-Drawer Chest with Wood Pulls (1941-42) Size of top 32" x 19". Height 46". ($850-1,000)

Coronet

The Russian born Count de Sakhnoffsky (also known for his automotive designs of the 1930s and 1940s) had a major impact on Heywood-Wakefield's Modern furniture. The Coronet group, notes the company, "features those inimitable Sakhnoffsky swept-back curves and those flowing streamline motifs for which he has become so justly famous."

C 3932 – Chest (1941-42) Top 33" x 20". Height 47". ($1,500-1,800)

C 3934 – Vanity Base (1941-42) A dual purpose piece which also serves as a kneehole desk. Size of top 44" x 18". Height 29". ($1,150-1,250)

C 3735 – Hanging Mirror (1940-42) Glass size 36" in diameter. ($200-250)

C 3535 A – Side Chair (1939-43) Seat 16 ½" x 16 ½". Height of back 17". ($375-475)

C 3931 – Dresser Base (1941-42) Size of dresser top 44" x 20". Height 34". ($1,250-1,350)

C 3931-933 – Dresser with Attached Mirror (1941-42) Glass size 42" x 28". ($1,250-1,500)

C 3535 A – Side Chair (1939-43) Seat 16 ½" x 16 ½". Height of back 17". ($375-475)

C 3930 – Bed (1941-42) Available in 3' 3" and 4' 6" sizes. ($500-600)

C 3938 – Night Stand (1941-42) Size of top 14" x 15". Height 25 ½". ($500-550)

C 3936 – Vanity (1941-42) Size of top 53" x 18". Height of base 22". Overall height of vanity 65". Mirror has plate which measures 38" wide and 44" high. Lower plate in base measures 10" x 19". Vanity is fitted with glass powder shelf between the piers. ($1,550-1,800)

C 3937 – Vanity Bench (1941-42) Fitted with revolving top. Seat 20" in diameter. ($350-450)

C 3767 C – Reading Chair (1940-42) Seat 22" x 22". Height of back 24". Reversible, spring filled seat cushion. Spring filled back. Not available in leather or imitation leather. ($1,150-1,250)

Niagara

A bow-knot motif in the drawer pulls and bases is a central design feature of this "swanky" bedroom set designed by Leo Jiranek.

C 3920 – Bed (1941-42) Available in 3' 3" and 4' 6" sizes. ($500-600)

C 3921-923 – Dresser with Attached Mirror (1941-42) This is dresser shown in large view. Size of dresser top 42" x 20". Height of dresser base 34". Mirror size 40" x 28". ($1,250-1,400)

C 3921 – Dresser Base (1941-42) This is the separate base without any mirror attached. ($1,000-1,250)

C 3928 – Night Stand (1941-42) Size of top 14" square. Height 25 ½". ($450-550)

C 3921-725 – Dresser with Attached Mirror (1941-42) This is dresser shown in single, silhouette view below. Size of dresser top 42" x 20". Height of dresser base 34". Mirror glass is 30" in diameter. ($1,250-1,450)

C 3922 – Chest (1941-42) Size of top 33" x 20". Height 47". ($1,350-1,550)

C 3596 A – Side Chair (1940-44) Seat 16" x 16". Height of back 16". ($200-225)

C 3924 – Vanity Base (1941-42) This is a 5-drawer vanity base which may also be used as a kneehole desk. Top measures 44" x 18". Height 29". ($1,150-1,250)

C 3923 – Hanging Mirror (1941-42) This is separate, hanging mirror shown over vanity. Size of glass 40" x 28". ($175-225)

C 3926 – **Vanity** (1941-42) Size of top 53" x 18". Height of base 23". Overall height of vanity 61". Mirror has plate which measures 52" x 38". Lower plate in base measures 22" x 19". Vanity is fitted with glass powder shelf between piers. ($1,250-1,350)

C 3927 – **Vanity Bench** (1941-42) Fitted with revolving top. Seat 20" wide. Height of seat from floor 17". ($450-550)

Miami

Also designed by Jiranek, the Miami bedroom suite combines "a note of luxury with simple effective design motifs such as flared bases; sleek bar pulls; and softened streamlined edges."

C 3910 – Bed (1941-42) Available in 3' 3" and 4' 6" sizes. ($500-600)

C 3918 – Night Stand (1941-42) Size of top 13" x 14". Height 25 ½". Fitted with drawer at top and hinged, storage compartment in base. ($300-350)

C 3911 – Dresser Base (1941-42) Size of top 42" x 19". Height 34". ($800-950)

C 3913 – Hanging Mirror (1941-42) Plate size 34" x 22". ($200-225)

C 3915 – Hanging Mirror (1941-42) This mirror is similar in style to the C 3913 except that it has a wood frame on one side of mirror only. Glass measures 32" x 26" (not shown). ($200-225)

C 3715 A – Side Chair (1940-42) Seat 16" x 15". Height of back 16 ½". ($125-150)

C 3916 – Vanity (1941-42) Size of top 46" x 18". Height of base 23". Overall height 56". Mirror size 36" x 34". ($900-1,000)

C 3917 – Vanity Bench (1941-42) Top measures 24" x 15". Height 17". ($250-275)

C 3912 – 4-Drawer Chest (1941-42) Size of top 32" x 19". Height 43". ($1,000-1,100)

C 3911-725 – Dresser with Attached Mirror (1941-42) This is dresser with attached mirror shown in small view at left. Size of dresser top 42" x 19". Height 34". Mirror is 30" in diameter. ($1,000-1,200)

C 3914 – Vanity Base (1941-42) This is the separate vanity base with 4 drawers. Top of base measures 46" x 18". Height of base 23". ($750-900)

C 3735 – Hanging Mirror (1940-42) Glass size, 36" in diameter. ($200-250)

Catalina

Another "traffic builder," Catalina was noted as the lowest priced Modern bedroom of its time. A 1941 article in *Shop News* (the company's employee newsletter) described this set as "simple and effective without being extreme."

C 3904 – Vanity Base (1941-42) This 4-drawer vanity base has a 42" x 18" top. Height 25". ($550-650)

C 3903 – Hanging Mirror (1941-42) Size of glass 28" x 22". ($175-200)

C 3907 – Vanity Bench (1941-42) Padded top measures 22" x 16". Height 16". ($200-225)

C 3902 – Chest (1941-42) Size of top 32" x 19". Height 43". ($550-650)

C 3901-725 – Dresser with Attached Mirror (1941-42) This is dresser with attached mirror in silhouette view shown at right. Size of dresser top 40" x 19". Height 34". Mirror is 30" in diameter. ($550-650)

C 3900 – Bed (1941-42) Available in 3' 3" and 4' 6" sizes. ($300-400)

C 3901 – Dresser Base (1941-42) Top measures 40" x 19". Height 34". ($500-600)

C 3903 – Hanging Mirror (1941-42) Glass size 28" x 22". ($175-200)

C 3908 – Night Stand (1941-42) Size of top 14" x 13". Height 25". ($200-225)

C 3765 C – Arm Chair (1940-42) Seat 22" x 20". Height of back 16". ($750-900)

C 3904-923 – Vanity with Attached Mirror (1941-42) This is complete vanity shown in the small view below. The vanity base has a 42" x 18" top and is 25" high. The mirror plate is 28" x 40". ($550-650)

Shown in the 1941-42 catalog, this pair of beds was evidently not connected with any of the matched bedroom suites.

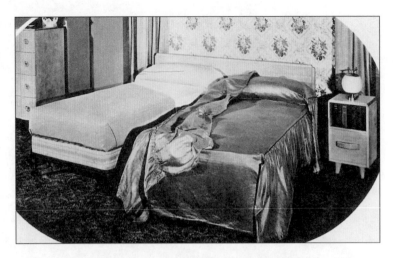

C 3770 – Pair of Attached Beds (1941-42) This is a popular modern piece which saves considerable space in the bedroom. It consists of two pivoting metal frames (on coasters) which swing out from headboard. These frames accommodate standard, twin size (3'3") springs and mattresses. The headboard is made in one piece. The number given above covers the complete unit. ($650-800)

Rio

Designed by Leo Jiranek, Rio was part of Heywood-Wakefield's Basic Line produced during the war years and featured "cross-strap" style wood pulls. A postwar redesign of this suite called Riviera was produced in 1947-48.

C 3790 – Bed
(1943-44) Available
in 3' 3" and 4' 6"
sizes. ($500-600)

C 3798 – Night Stand (1943-44) Top measures 13" x 13". Height 25 ½". ($300-400)

C 3792 – Chest (1943-44) Top measures 19" x 32". Height 45". ($1,000-1,100)

C 3791-795 – Dresser with Attached Mirror (1943-44) Width 42". Depth 20". Overall height 68". Plate in mirror measures 32" x 34". ($800-900)

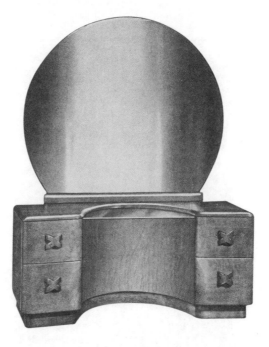

C 3796 – Deluxe Vanity (1943-44) Top measures 18" x 49". Base height 21 ½". Overall height 61 ½". ($750-850)

C 3797 – Revolving Top Bench (1943-44) Pouffe with revolving top fitted with circular spring unit. Diameter 20". Height 17". ($250-300)

Victory

Victory was the second of the Basic Line bedroom groups. No photograph could be located showing these pieces in a room setting.

C 4140 – **Bed** (1943-44) Available in 3' 3" and 4' 6" sizes. ($375-425)

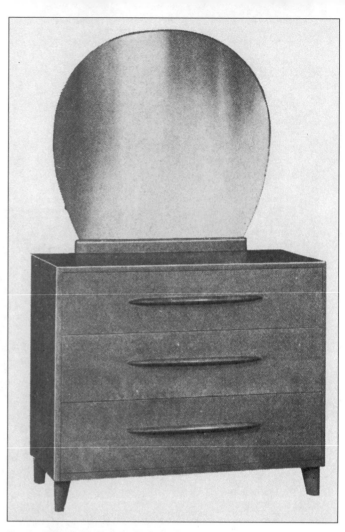

C 4141-795 – **Dresser with Attached Mirror** (1943-44) Width 40". Depth 19". Overall height 68". Plate in mirror measures 32" x 34". ($650-750)

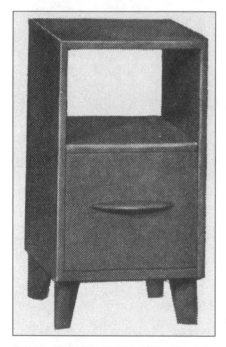

C 4148 – **Night Stand** (1943-44) Top 13" x 14". Height 24". Opening fits midget radio. Compartment has hinged door. ($300-350)

C 4142 – **Chest** (1943-44) Top measures 19" x 32". Height 42 ½". ($750-850)

C 4141 – Dresser Base (1943-44) Dresser base only, top 19" x 40". Height 33 ½". ($500-550)

C 4143 – Hanging Mirror (1943-44) Plate measures 22" x 28". ($175-225)

C 4146 – Complete Vanity (1943-44) Top of four drawer vanity base (C 4144) measures 18" x 44". Height of base 25". Mirror measures 28" x 34". ($700-800)

C 4147 – Vanity Bench (1943-44) Upholstered slip seat top measures 22" x 16". Height 16". ($200-250)

1950s – The Modern Years

Bedroom Suites

This gallery of 1950s bedroom suites illustrates each of the matched sets from that era. (Not all pieces from a set may be included in these room setting photographs.) It is followed by separate sections showing individual pictures of all 1950s beds, night stands, dressers/chests, and vanities, with each of those functional sections also organized according to suite names.

Encore
Among the most well-known of Heywood-Wakefield's bedroom suites, Encore was a large group with a greater selection of pieces than had been available for earlier suites. It was produced in an early version from circa 1948 to 1953 (shown here), and in a later, redesigned version starting in 1956.

Kohinoor
Featuring an interesting combination of concave and convex drawer fronts, the Kohinoor suite was designed by Ernest Herrmann and named after a legendary diamond presented to Queen Victoria of Britain in 1850.

Trophy

A *Shop News* article from August 1951 featured these four photographs of the Trophy suite. Introduced at the Chicago and New York furniture markets of that year, the suite won "strong dealer acclaim," reports the article. Design elements included clean lines, recessed drawer pulls, and a shadowbox case treatment. (Note: These images of the Trophy suite were the only ones available for use in this book, therefore individual pieces are not shown in the subsequent sections on beds, night stands, dressers/chests, and vanities.)

M 576 – **Vanity** (1951-52) ($1,050-1,200)

M 572 – **4-Drawer Chest** (1951-52) ($1,100-1,200)

M 570 – **Bed** (1951-52) ($450-500)

M 574-575 – **Mr. and Mrs. Dresser with Attached Mirror** (1951-52) ($1,150-1,250)

M 571-573 – **3-Drawer Dresser with Attached Mirror** (1951-52) ($1,050-1,150)

Sculptura

An especially elegant bedroom set, Sculptura was characterized by "folded-ribbon" drawer fronts with built-in pulls. The case pieces sat flush to the floor rather than on legs. Catalog copy was effusive in its praise for Sculptura, calling it "truly an example of sculpture performed on woodworking machines by skilled craftsmen."

Harmonic

The growing trend toward more angular lines is evident with Harmonic, a bedroom group that featured corresponding dining room pieces. Reporting on new patterns introduced at the winter furniture markets, *Shop News* of February 1954 had this to say about Harmonic: "Outstanding in the case pieces is the absence of protruding drawer pulls, the high bracket feet, and the design itself, the ultimate in modern styling."

Cadence

Angular lines are even more prominent in Cadence, a group designed by Ernest Herrmann. The drawers feature a beveled, three-dimensional look, with metal hardware (drawer pulls). The type of metal used for the drawer pulls varied according to the finish applied: pieces ordered in Wheat, Champagne, or Sable came with round pulls made of polished brass with white enamel centers, while pieces ordered in Sherry came with oblong shaped pewter pulls. (The same finish/drawer pull combinations applied to the corresponding Cadence dining room pieces as well.)

Tempo

Another of the more angular styled suites, Tempo was produced in 1955 and used brass trimmed, baton-shaped drawer pulls made of black walnut wood to contrast with the otherwise light finish.

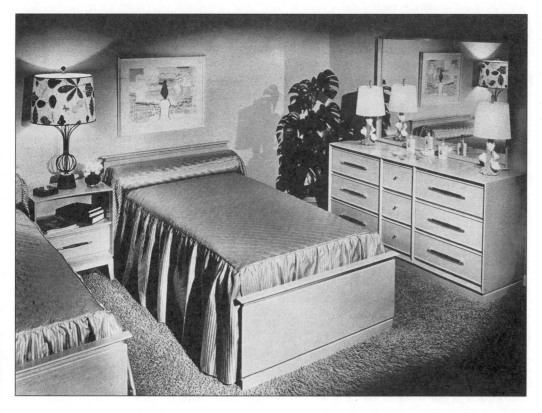

Dakar

Although still part of the Modern line as shown in Heywood-Wakefield catalogs, Dakar represented a significant departure from the more classically designed, blond colored Modern. Designed by Ernest Herrmann, this line was made of Mahogany rather than birch and was characterized by an "elliptical or leaf-shaped machine carving on the drawer fronts and headboard beds."

Encore

In 1956, Heywood-Wakefield gave the long running Encore line an actual "encore," introducing a redesign of this popular bedroom suite that featured a "lower, longer silhouette." Key case pieces (chest, double dresser, and triple dresser) were available in either "to-the-floor" or "off-the-floor" designs. Company literature emphasized the classic style of these later Encore pieces: "These new bedroom Encore pieces maintain the basic styling so characteristic of Heywood Modern. The soft edges, sleek wood pulls, and simple design are exclusive features in styling motif...Made of solid Birch wood and selected Birch drawer bottoms."

Symphonic

A late 1950s bedroom suite characterized by recessed, built-in drawer pulls with a decorative scroll motif around the outside. Unlike some of the more angular styled lines of this era, Symphonic pieces featured the "characteristic H-W soft curved edges."

Beds and Headboards

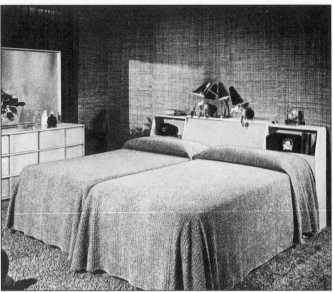

Encore

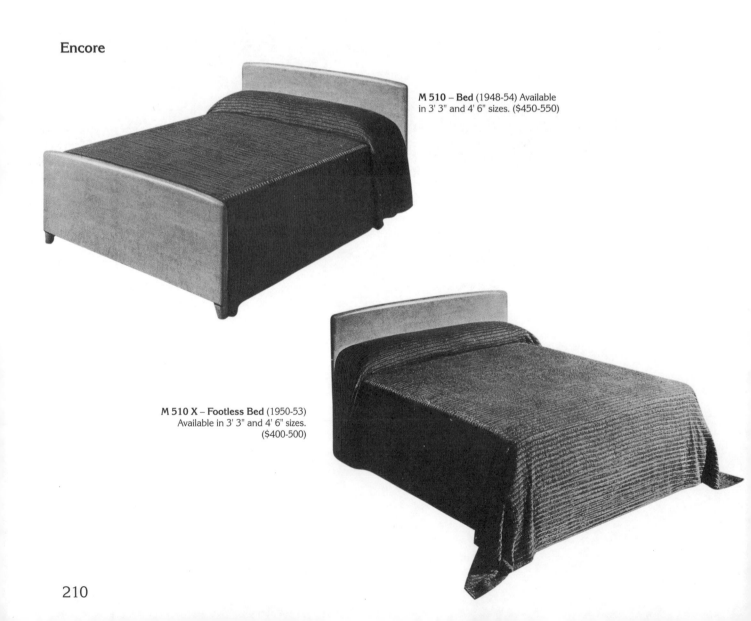

M 510 – Bed (1948-54) Available in 3' 3" and 4' 6" sizes. ($450-550)

M 510 X – Footless Bed (1950-53) Available in 3' 3" and 4' 6" sizes. ($400-500)

M 520 – Shelf Headboard Bed (1952-53) Available in 3' 3" and 4' 6" sizes. Overall length of single headboard 40 ½", of double headboard 55 ½". Overall height 34 ½". Shelf height 32 ½" to tie in with wall pieces. Fitted with Seng frame equipped with pin hinges so that metal frame can be swung in either direction or removed completely. ($375-475)

M 540 – Utility Headboard (1952-53) Available in 3' 3" and 4' 6" sizes. The headboards have three compartments fitted with two solid wood, ribbed sliding door panels. Equipped with Seng steel bed frames on easy rolling, self-lubricating casters. Fitted with two removable pin hinges which permit swinging the bed from either way. Frame can be permanently fastened to headboard. Double headboard is 55 ½" wide, 9" deep, and 40" high. Single headboard 27 ¼" wide, 9" deep, and 40" high. ($450-550)

M 530 – Bed (1950-53) Available in 3' 3" and 4' 6" sizes. ($800-1,000)

M 540 (6' 6") – Double Utility Headboard (1950-53) Each twin headboard has three compartments fitted with two solid wood, ribbed sliding door panels. Equipped with Seng steel bed frames on easy rolling, self lubricating casters. Double headboard consists of two single headboards clamped together; can be sold separately as twin beds. Headboard is 81" wide, 9" deep, and 40" high. ($450-550)

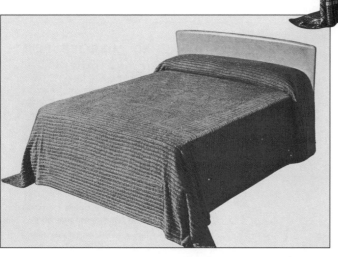

M 530 X – Footless Bed (1950-53) Available in 3' 3" and 4' 6" sizes. ($600-800)

M 780 (4' 6") – **Cabinet Utility Headboard** (1952-55) The headboard unit is 82" wide overall, including the built-on night stands. It is 11" deep and 32 ½" high…the same height as many H-W wall pieces. Fitted with a Seng frame equipped with pin hinges so that metal frame can be swung in either direction or removed completely. The built-on night stands have a drop door at the top that levels into a shelf and an adjustable shelf below. This pattern is not made in the 3' 3" size. ($800-1,000)

M 790 – **Utility Headboard** (1954-55) Available in 3' 3" and 4' 6" sizes. Shelf headboard has three compartments and two sliding, solid wood door panels. Twin headboard is 40 ½" wide, 37" high, and 10" deep; the double size is 55 ½" wide. The metal frame that supports the mattress is fitted with pin hinges which permits the frame to be swung either left or right, or removed completely from the headboard. ($450-550)

M 790 (6' 6") – **Double Utility Headboard** (1953-55) One-piece headboard is 81" wide, 37" high, and 11" deep. Closed center section has sliding doors and open end sections accommodate books, small radio, and other beside accessories. ($1,250-1,500)

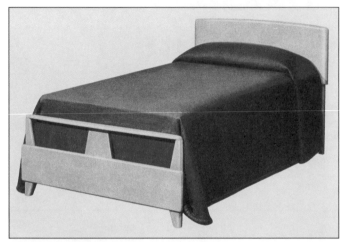

M 930 – **Bed** (1954) Available in 3' 3" and 4' 6" sizes. ($450-500)

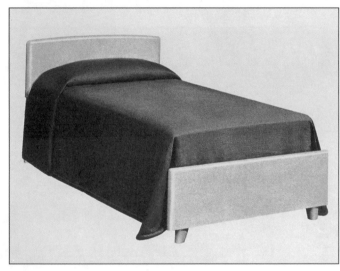

M 920 – **Bed** (1955) Available in 3' 3" and 4' 6" sizes. ($375-475)

Kohinoor

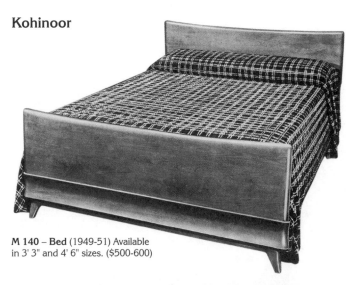

M 140 – Bed (1949-51) Available
in 3' 3" and 4' 6" sizes. ($500-600)

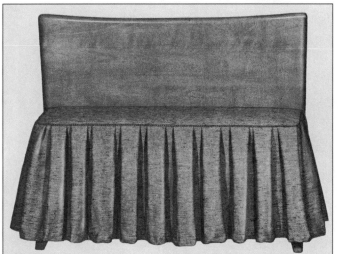

M 140 X – Footless Bed (1949-51) Available in 3' 3" and 4' 6" sizes. ($400-500)

Sculptura

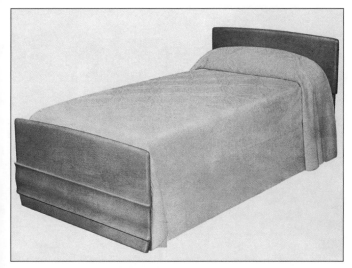

M 770 – Bed (1952-58) Available in 3' 3" and 4' 6" sizes. ($550-650)

M 770 H – Footless Bed (1952-58) Available in 3' 3" and 4' 6" sizes. Fitted with
Seng or Harvard adjustable metal bed frame. ($450-550)

M 770 (6' 6") – Headboard Bed (1956) Headboard measures 83" wide x 35 ½"
high. Fitted with two Seng or Harvard metal frames. ($450-550)

Harmonic

M 910 – Bed (1954) Available in 3' 3" and 4' 6" sizes.
Headboard height 35"; footboard height 18". ($450-550)

Cadence

M 1110 (6' 6") – **Double Tambour Footless Bed** (1955-59) Headboard has
tambour door single-shelf compartment at each end. Double headboard is
112" wide, 14 ½" deep, 32" high. Fitted with two Seng or Harvard metal frames
which swing apart easily. ($800-1,000)

M 1100 – Bed (1955-59) Available in 3' 3" and 4' 6" sizes.
Headboard height 32", footboard height 18". ($650-750)

M 1110 (4' 6") –
Tambour Footless Bed
(1955-59) Headboard
has tambour door
single-shelf compart-
ment at each end. One
piece headboard is 89
½" wide, 14 ¼" deep,
32" high. Fitted with
Seng or Harvard metal
frame. This bed is also
available with footboard
as M 1110 4/6 X. ($800-
1,000)

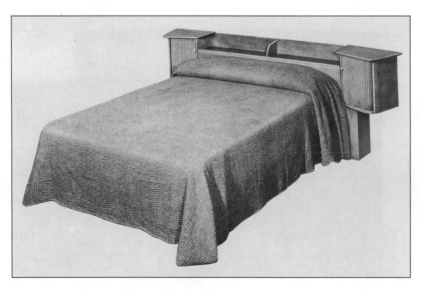

Tempo

M 730 – Bed (1955) Available in 3' 3"
and 4' 6" sizes. Height of headboard
31"; of footboard 18". ($500-600)

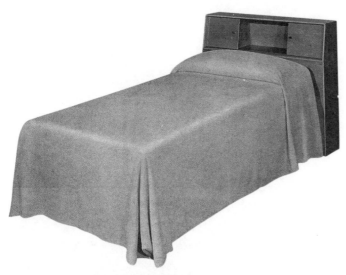

M 740 – Utility Headboard Bed (1955) Available in 3' 3" and 4' 6" sizes. Fitted
with two sliding doors. Twin headboard is 42 1/3" wide; double size is 57 ½"
wide, height 37", depth 10 ¼". Fitted with adjustable metal frame. ($400-600)

M 740 (6' 6") – **Double Utility Headboard** (1955) This double headboard is
made up of two M 740 single beds clamped together at the rear. Headboard is
85" wide, 10 ¼" deep, and 37" high. Fitted with metal bed frames that can be
attached or hinged to swing apart. ($600-800)

Dakar

M 1710 – Panel Bed (1955-56) Available in 3' 3" and 4' 6" sizes.
Headboard is 32" high; footboard is 18" high. ($600-700)

M 1720 – Utility Headboard Bed
(1955-56) Available in 3' 3", 4' 6", and
6' 6" sizes. Twin headboard is 42 ½"
wide x 37" high; double is 57 ½" wide x
37" high. 6' 6" size is made up of two
twin sizes. ($500-700)

M 1730 – Utility Headboard Bed with End Compartments
(1955-56) Available in 4' 6" and 6' 6" sizes. End compartments
attached to headboard. Solid, square brass gallery. Double size
is 91 ½" wide x 37" high; 6' 6" size is 119" wide x 37" high.
($700-1,000)

Encore

M 1500 – Bed (1956-62) Available in 3' 3" and 4' 6" sizes. Also available without footboard as M 1500 3/3H or 4/6H. ($450-550)

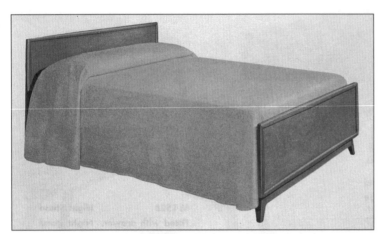

M 1510 – Panel Bed (1956) Available in 3' 3" and 4' 6" sizes. This bed is also available without footboard as M 1510 3/3H or 4/6H. ($450-550)

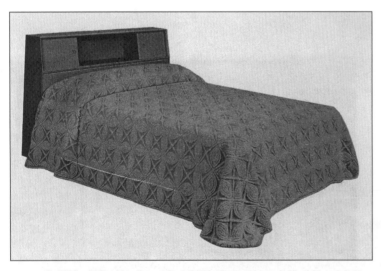

M 1520 – Utility Headboard Bed (1956-62) Available in 3' 3", 4' 6", and 6' 6" sizes. The 6' 6" size consists of two 3' 3" headboards with attaching device for holding the headboards together. The 3' 3" and 4' 6" beds are also available with footboards as M 1520 3/3 X and M 1520 4/6 X. ($400-500)

M 1530 (4' 6") – **Utility Headboard Bed** (1956) Headboard is fitted with two open front end compartments. Bed has Seng or Harvard metal frame. Headboard is 101 ½" wide, 37" high, 10 ¼" deep. The bed is also available with footboard as M 1530 4/6 X or M 1530 4/6 X WD. ($600-700)

M 1540 (4' 6") – **Cabinet Utility Headboard Bed** (1956-58) Headboard has built-in night stands. Night stands have drop doors. Fitted with Seng or Harvard metal frame. ($900-1,100)

M 1560 – Bed (1958-62) Available in 3' 3" and 4' 6" sizes. Also available without footboard as M 1560 3/3H and M 1560 4/6H. ($375-475)

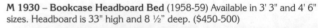

M 1930 – Bookcase Headboard Bed (1958-59) Available in 3' 3" and 4' 6" sizes. Headboard is 33" high and 8 ½" deep. ($450-500)

M 1940 (4'6") – **Utility Headboard Bed** (1958-61) Headboard has open cabinet at each end fitted with drawer. Headboard is 91" wide, 32" high and 12" deep. ($750-900)

M 1920 H – **Paneled Headboard Bed** (1962-63) Available in 6' 6" size only. Headboard measures 82 ½" wide x 37 ½" high. No footboard. One-piece paneled headboard has full-length cap. Headboard is fitted with two "Swing-Away" metal bed frames which can be "locked" together for a "King-size" mattress. ($650-800)

Night Stands/Night Tables

Encore

M 518 – **Night Stand** (1948-55) Fitted with adjustable shelf. Top measures 15" x 14". Height 26". ($350-425)

M 538 – **Night Stand** (1950-55) Fitted with drawer. Open back for telephone or radio wires. Tier top measures 19" x 13". Overall width 20"; overall depth 16". Height 26". ($450-550)

Kohinoor

M 148 – **Night Stand** (1949-51) Size of top 20" x 16". Height 24". ($450-550)

Sculptura

M 778 – Night Stand (1952-58) Fitted with drawer. Overall width 20". Overall depth 16". Height 24". ($650-750)

Tempo

M 738 – Night Stand (1955) Fitted with drawer and shelf. Top measures 21" x 16". Height 25". ($250-350)

Dakar

M 1718 – Night Stand (1955-56) Fitted with solid Mahogany sliding panel doors. Top measures 21" wide x 16 ½" deep. Height 24 ½". ($250-350)

Harmonic

M 918 – Night Stand (1954) Fitted with drawer and shelf. Top measures 20" x 18". Height 25 ½". ($450-550)

Encore

M 1508 – Night Stand (1956) Drop-front conceals storage space fitted with tray-drawer. Back wall is white Plastone. Top measures 22" x 17 ½". Height 26". ($300-350)

Cadence

M 1108 – Night Stand (1955-59) Fitted with drawer and shelf. Top measures 24" x 18 ½". Height 25". ($175-200)

M 1518 – Night Stand/Pier Cabinet (1956) Equipped with three drawers. Top measures 22" x 17". Height 26". ($450-550)

M 1528 – Night Stand (1956-62) Fitted with drawer. Night stand measures 20" wide, 15" deep, 25" high. ($375-450)

M 1538 – Night Table (1958) Fitted with one drawer. Overall size is 19" wide, 15" deep, 25" high. ($450-525)

Dressers and Chests

Note that some dressers that came with or without attached mirrors are shown here with the dresser alone.

Encore

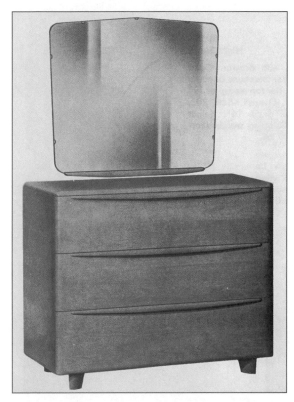

Symphonic

M 1938 – Night Table (1958) Fitted with one drawer. Has closed back. Overall size of night table is 19" wide, 15" deep, 25" high. ($350-400)

M 511-515 – 3-Drawer Dresser with Attached Mirror (1948-50) Size of top 42" wide by 19" deep. Height 34". Shield-shaped mirror has 34" wide by 28" high plate glass. ($850-950)

M 512 – 4-Drawer Chest (1950) Top measures 32" x 19". Height 42". ($1,050-1,200)

M 521-525 – 4-Drawer Dresser with Attached Mirror (1950-55) Top measures 42" wide by 19" deep. Height 34". Fitted with pin tray in top drawer. Plate glass size, 40" wide by 28" high. ($800-1,000)

M 522 – 5-Drawer Chest (1950-55) Top measures 34" x 19". Height 46". ($1,250-1,450)

M 524 – Mr. & Mrs. Dresser (1950-55) Top measures 54" wide by 19" deep. Height 34". ($1,150-1,350)

M 529-575 – Triple Dresser with Attached Mirror (1952-55) Top measures 60" x 19". Height 34". Mirror has plate glass measuring 50" x 34". ($2,500-2,800)

M 532 – Double Chest (1954-55) This double chest has 7 drawers. Top measures 44" x 19". Height 46". ($2,250-2,650)

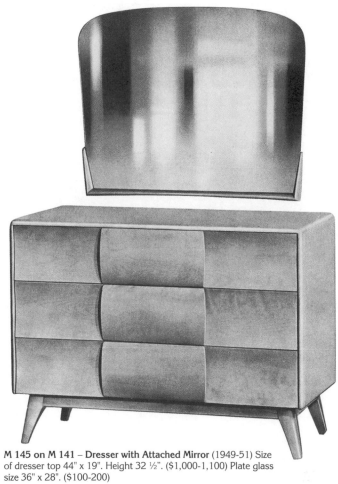

M 145 on M 141 – Dresser with Attached Mirror (1949-51) Size of dresser top 44" x 19". Height 32 ½". ($1,000-1,100) Plate glass size 36" x 28". ($100-200)

Kohinoor

M 142 – Chest (1949-51) Size of top 34" x 19". Height 45". ($1,250-1,350)

M 144-525 – Mr. & Mrs. Dresser with Attached Mirror (1949-51) Dresser top measures 56" x 19". Height 32 ½". ($1,350-1,500) Plate glass size 40" x 28". ($100-200)

M 149 on M 141 – Dresser with Deck Top (1949-51) Dresser measures 44" wide, 19" deep, 32 ½" high. Deck top measures 42" wide, 17 ½" deep, 10 ½" high. Overall height 43". ($1,700-2,000)

Sculptura

M 771-573 – Dresser with Attached Mirror (1952-54) Dresser top is 46" x 19". Height 31". Attached mirror has plate glass 34" wide x 32" high. Overall height of base and mirror 63". ($1,050-1,150)

M 781 on M 771 – Deck Top on Dresser (1952) Single dresser measures 46" x 19". Height 31". Deck top measures 42" x 16". Height 19". Overall height of base and deck 50". ($1,550-1,800)

M 772 – Chest (1952-59) Top measures 38" x 19". Height 39". ($1,250-1,350)

M 774-575 – Mr. & Mrs. Dresser with Attached Mirror (1952-58) Top measures 56" x 19". Height 31". Plate glass size 50" wide by 34" high. ($1,250-1,500)

M 779-575 – Triple Dresser with Attached Mirror (1952-58) Top measures 62" x 19". Height 31". Mirror has 50" x 34" plate glass. ($2,250-2,500)

M 792 – 5-Drawer Chest (1953-59) Size of top 38" x 19". Height 48". ($1,500-1,700)

Harmonic

M 911 – 3-Drawer Dresser (1954-55) Top measures 46" x 19". Height 31". ($1,050-1,150)

M 912 – 5-Drawer Chest (1954-55) Top measures 38" x 19". Height 45 ½". ($1,250-1,350)

M 914 – Mr. and Mrs. Dresser (1954) This 6-drawer double dresser has a top that measures 60" x 19". It stands 31" high. ($1,250-1,350)

Cadence

Note that most of the case pieces for this line have large overhanging tops, except for the M 1111 and M 1112, which have flush tops (allowing them to be butted together when placed side by side).

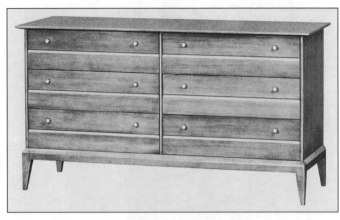

M 1104 – Double Dresser (1955-59) Fitted with six drawers. Top measures 59" x 20 ½". Height 31 ½". ($500-600)

M 1101-1103 – 4-Drawer Dresser with Attached Mirror (1955-56) Fitted with four drawers. Top measures 48" x 20 ½". Height 31 ½". Attached mirror has 40" x 28" plate glass. Overall height of base and mirror is 63 ½". ($600-700)

M 1109-1105 – Triple Dresser with Attached Mirror (1955-59) Fitted with nine drawers. Top measures 65" x 20 ½". Height 31 ½". Attached mirror has 50" x 34" plate glass. Overall height of dresser and mirror is 67 ¼". ($700-800)

M 1102 – 5-Drawer Chest (1955-59) Fitted with five drawers. Top measures 41" x 20 ½". Height 44 ½". Two removable shirt partitions in second drawers. ($500-600)

M 1111 – **3-Drawer Dresser** (1955-56) Fitted with three drawers. Top measures 38" x 19". Height 31 ½". ($400-500)

M 1116 – **Dresser/Desk** (1958-59) Fitted with four drawers. Top measures 54" x 20 ½". Height is 30". M 116 P is same piece but has white plastic top. ($350-450)

Tempo

M 1112 – **4-Drawer Chest** (1955-56) Fitted with four drawers. Top measures 38" x 19". Height 39". Two removable shirt partitions in second drawer. ($500-600)

M 1119 – **Tambour Chest** (1955-59) Two Tambour door compartments are fitted with pull-out drawer tray in each; ample space provided below trays. Chest has three full-length drawers. Top measures 41" x 20 ½". Height 45 ½". ($600-700)

M 731-525 – **Dresser with Attached Mirror** (1955) Fitted with three drawers. Top measures 46" x 19". Height 31". Attached mirror has 40" x 28" plate glass. Overall height of base and mirror is 61 ½". ($650-800)

M 732 – 4-Drawer Chest (1955) Fitted with four drawers. Top measures 38" x 19". Height 38 ½". Two removable shirt partitions. ($550-650)

M 742 – 5-Drawer Chest (1955) Fitted with five drawers. Top measures 38" x 19". Height 46 ½". Two removable shirt partitions. ($650-750)

M 734 – Double Dresser (1955)
Fitted with six drawers. Top measures 56" x 19". Height 31". ($550-650)

M 739 – Triple Dresser (1955) Fitted with nine drawers. Top measures 62" x 19". Height 31". ($650-750)

Dakar

M 1712 – 4-Drawer Chest (1955-56) Top measures 38" wide x 19" deep. Height 40 ½". Fitted with two shirt partitions in second drawer. ($350-450)

M 1719-1715 – Triple Dresser with Attached Mirror (1955-56) Top measures 64" wide x 19" deep. Height of dresser 32". Mirror has plate glass 50" x 34". ($500-600)

M 1714-1715 – Double Dresser with Attached Mirror (1955-56) Top measures 58" wide x 19" deep. Height of dresser 32". Mirror has plate glass 50" x 34". Mirror attached with two-bracket, adjustable, tilting standard. ($500-600)

M 1714 W – Double Dresser with Vanity/Desk Drawer (1955-56) This illustration shows the vanity/desk drawer fitted to the double dresser M 1714. ($600-700)

M 1722 – 5-Drawer Chest (1955-56) Top measures 42" wide x 19" deep. Height 45". Fitted with two shirt partitions in second middle drawer. ($450-550)

M 1512 – 5-Drawer Chest (1956-60) Fitted with five drawers. Top measures 36" x 19". Height is 44". ($1,150-1,250)

Encore

M 1509 – Cane Door Chest (1956-59) Fitted with two cane door compartments. The left compartment has two trays and the right is equipped with an adjustable shelf. Chest measures 40" wide, 19" deep, 50" high. ($650-750)

M 1531 on M 1521 – 3-Drawer Deck on Single Dresser (1956) M 1531 deck is fitted with three full length drawers with center partition in each drawer. Deck is 39 ½" wide, 17" deep, 19" high. Single dresser has four drawers. Dresser top measures 42" x 19". Height 32". Overall height of deck and dresser is 51". ($1,000-1,250)

M 1536 on M 1521 – Tambour Deck Utility Cabinet on Single Dresser
(1956) M 1536 Deck Cabinet is fitted with two Tambour sliding doors and
contour-front adjustable shelf. Deck is 39 ½" wide, 17" deep and 19" high.
Dresser has four drawers. Top measures 42" x 19", height 32". Overall height of
deck and dresser is 51". ($1,200-1,300)

M 1514-1525 – Double Dresser with Attached Mirror (1956-60)
Fitted with six drawers. Top measures 56" x 19". Height 32". Mirror has
plate glass 34" x 52". Overall height of dresser and mirror is 68".
($1,150-1,350)

M 1522 – 5-Drawer Chest (1956-62) Fitted with five drawers. Top measures
38" x 19". Height is 44". ($1,200-1,350)

M 1524-1515 – Double Dresser with Attached Mirror (1956-62) Fitted with
eight drawers. Top measures 56" x 19". Height of dresser is 32". Mirror has plate
glass 32" x 44". Overall height of mirror and dresser 67". ($1,150-1,250)

M 1532 – 4-Drawer Chest
(1958) Fitted with four drawers. Second drawer is extra deep; has removable shirt partition. Top measures 34" x 18". Height 43". ($1,000-1,100)

M 1582 – 5-Drawer Chest
(1958) Fitted with five drawers. Third drawer has removable shirt partition. Top measures 34" x 18". Height is 43". ($1,050-1,150)

M 1519-1525 – Triple Dresser with Attached Mirror (1956-60) Fitted with nine drawers. Center top drawer has sculptured wood pin tray. Top measures 62" x 19". Height of dresser is 32". Mirror has plate glass 34" x 52"; overall 36" x 54". Overall height of dresser and mirror 68". ($1,750-2,000)

M 1529-1525 – Triple Dresser with Attached Mirror (1956-62) Fitted with twelve drawers. Center top drawer has sculptured wood pin tray. Dresser has four swivel caster wheels. Top is 62" x 19". Height of dresser 32". Mirror has plate glass 34" x 52"; overall 36" x 54". Overall height of dresser and mirror 68". ($1,750-2,000)

M 1539-1535 – Triple Dresser with Attached Mirror (1958) Fitted with nine drawers. Top measures 58" x 18". Height 31". Mirror has plate glass 40" x 28". Overall height of mirror and dresser is 62". ($1,650-1,850)

**M 1511 –
Bachelor's Chest**
(1958) Fitted with
four drawers. Top
measures 30" x 18".
Height is 31". ($700-
800)

**M 1934-1533 –
Double Dresser with
Attached Mirror**
(1958) Fitted with six
drawers. Top
measures 52" x 18".
Height is 31". Hanging
mirror has plate glass
36" x 28". Mirror may
be hung vertically as
shown, or horizon-
tally—it is fitted with
hanging clips for use
with wire. ($900-
1,000)

M 1534-1533 – Double Dresser with Attached Mirror (1958) Fitted
with six drawers. Top measures 52" x 18". Height 31". Mirror has plate
glass 36" x 28". Overall size of mirror and frame is 38" x 30". Overall
height of dresser and mirror is 62". ($1,050-1,150)

Symphonic

M 1932 – 4-Drawer Chest
(1958) Fitted with four
drawers. Second drawer is
extra deep for shirts;
removable partition. Chest
top measures 34" x 18".
Height is 43". ($850-950)

M 1939-1535 – Triple Dresser with Attached Mirror (1958) Fitted with nine
drawers. Top measures 58" x 18". Height is 31". Mirror has plate glass 40" x 28".
Overall height of mirror and dresser is 62". ($1,150-1,250)

Encore

M 536 – Vanity (1950-53) Fitted with full length mirror, plate glass shelf, and pin tray in top drawer. Overall height 65". Wood pier measures 26" x 18". Overall width 54". Height of base 24". ($1,150-1,350)

M 537 – Vanity Bench (1950-53) Spring filled top measures 26" wide by 17" deep. Height 15". ($450-550)

M 516 – Vanity (1948-50) The 4-drawer base is a spacious 49" x 18". The overall vanity height is 60" which affords full length reflection. There is a plate glass shelf in the center. The mirror is shield-shaped plate glass that measures 38" x 42". ($800-900)

M 517 – Vanity Bench (1948-50) The vanity bench or pouffe has a spring filled top that measures 22" x 15". It stands 16" high. ($200-250)

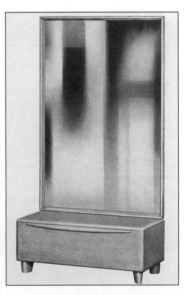

M 539-575 X – Blanket Chest with Attached Mirror (1952-54)

Blanket chest, M 539, is available without the attached mirror. It is 35 ½" wide x 15 ½" deep. Height 14". Fitted with full length drawer. ($1,550-1,800)

Kohinoor

M 586 – Deluxe Vanity (1953-55) Fitted with full length mirror and plate glass shelf. Overall height 62 ½". Overall width 50". Depth of base 18". Height of base 20". ($1,550-1,800)

M 546 – Desk-Vanity (1949) This Modern design styled to the Kohinoor bedroom grouping serves as both a vanity and desk. The base measures 50" x 22". The base height is 28". Height to top of pier 36". Overall height 54". Fitted with Tambour doors. Plate glass measures 38" wide by 26" high. ($2,750-3,000)

M 587 – Vanity Bench (1953-54) Spring-filled top measures 31" long by 25" wide. Height 15". ($450-550)

M 926 – Vanity/Desk (1955-56) Steam-bent drawer fronts. Top measures 50" x 22". Height 30". ($2,500-3,000)

M 146 – Deluxe Vanity (1949-51) Base measures 50" x 18". Height of base 23". Plate glass size 44" x 36". Overall height 58". ($1,000-1,200)

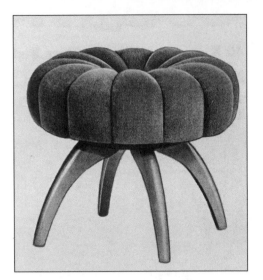

M 147 – Vanity Bench (1949-51) Revolving top measures 20" in diameter. Height 17". ($300-400)

Sculptura

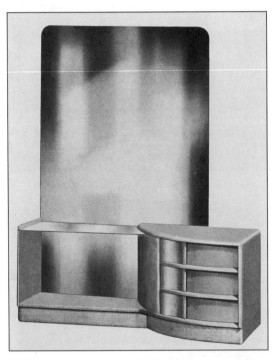

M 776 – Deluxe Vanity (1952-58) Plate glass, which extends to bottom shelf, measures 42" high x 38" wide. Plate glass shelf. Vanity base is 50" wide by 18" deep. Base height 20". ($1,150-1,350)

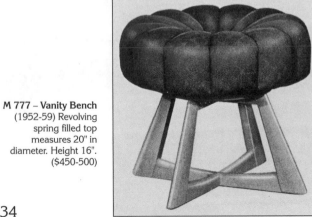

M 777 – Vanity Bench (1952-59) Revolving spring filled top measures 20" in diameter. Height 16". ($450-500)

Harmonic

M 916 – Desk/Vanity (1954) This desk/vanity is fully finished at the back and will not, therefore, accommodate an attached mirror. Size of top 44" x 19". Height 30". ($1,200-1,300)

Cadence

M 1106 – Desk/Vanity (1955-59) Top measures 48" x 24". Height 28 ½". Fitted with three drawers and shelf. Finished in back so that it may be placed away from the wall. ($300-400)

234

Tempo

M 923 on M 736 – Mirror on Desk/Vanity (1955) Fitted with two drawers and two shelves. Finished in back so that it may be placed away from the wall. Top measures 50" x 21". Height 28". ($500-650)

M 1716-M 1713 – Vanity (1955) The vanity section at the left has a white melamine plastic surface and a stationery box fitted with sliding doors of special white Plastone. It is hung to the chest with a brass bracket at the front and a brass plate at the back. The legs of the vanity can be pivoted to either side so that it can be hung at the left or right of any 32" high chest or dresser. This vanity is 32" wide x 23" deep. It is 32" high overall. The hanging mirror has a 30" x 24" plate glass. It is fitted with clips for hanging. It can be hung either vertically or horizontally over the vanity or 3-drawer chest. ($500-650)

Dakar

M 1717 – Vanity Bench (1955) The contour seat has a generous 25" x 18" top. It stands 18" high. ($200-225)

M 1711 – Vanity Chest (1955-56) This bachelor or bride-to-be chest can be used by itself, as shown, or it can be used with the M 1716 vanity section as illustrated next. Top measures 29 ½" wide x 19" deep. Height 32". ($350-450)

Bibliography

Books

Gertz, Harris. *Heywood-Wakefield*. Atglen, PA: Schiffer Publishing, Ltd., 2001.

Greenwood, Richard N. *The Five Heywood Brothers (1826-1951). A Brief History of the Heywood-Wakefield Company during 125 Years*. New York: The Newcomen Society in North America, 1951.

McMillian, Elizabeth. *Deco & Streamlined Architecture in L.A.* Atglen, PA: Schiffer Publishing, Ltd., 2004.

Rouland, Steve and Roger. *Heywood-Wakefield Modern Furniture*. Paducah, KY: Collector Books, 1995.

Catalogs (listed chronologically)

Modern Furniture by Heywood Wakefield (c. 1935 catalog)

Heywood-Wakefield Streamline Maple – Modern Furniture (1936 catalog)

Heywood-Wakefield Streamline Furniture (1937, 1938, and 1939 catalogs)

Streamline Modern by Heywood-Wakefield (1939, 1940, and c. 1941 brochures)

Modern Furniture by Heywood-Wakefield (1940 and 1940-41 catalog)

Heywood-Wakefield Basic Line of Streamline Modern Furniture (1943 poster style brochure)

Heywood-Wakefield's Revised Basic Line of Streamline Modern Furniture (1944 poster style brochure)

Modern Kohinoor Suite (c. 1949 fold out brochure)

Modern by Heywood-Wakefield (1950, 1951-52, 1952-53, 1953-54, 1954-55, 1955, and 1956 catalogs)

Modern by Heywood-Wakefield "Exclusive West Coast Patterns" (c. 1952 fold out brochure)

The "Harmonic" Bedroom (c. 1954 brochure)

The "Harmonic" Dining Room (c. 1954 brochure)

Modern Furniture by Heywood-Wakefield (1957-58 catalog)

Modern Upholstered Furniture, Occasional Chairs, Occasional Tables (1958 catalog)

Modern Cadence Furniture (1958-1959 catalog)

Modern – New Encore Bedroom (c. 1958 fold out brochure)

Modern Encore Furniture (1958-59, 1960-61, and 1962-63 catalogs)

Heywood-Wakefield Finishes and Identification

The "blond" color so characteristic of the furniture show-cased in this book (and so popular with those who favor mid-century looks for twenty-first century homes of today) was typically achieved through one of two finishes applied to the wood: Wheat or Champagne. Quite a few other finishes were used as well—as seen in the chronology and finish list below—yet Wheat and Champagne were far and away the two most enduring and popular. Harris Gertz, writing in *Heywood-Wakefield*, notes that the less desirable brown finishes are so out of character with the style of Modern furniture that the current value of pieces finished in this way is greatly reduced. Harris also notes that both Wheat and Champagne changed slightly over time, so early versions may be subtly different from later versions:

> Champagne particularly evolved from a mostly or-ange-amber tone in the 1940s to showing hints of pink in its orange hue in the 1950s. By the late 1950s, Champagne was more overtly pink. These three versions of Champagne do not match each other exactly, although they are all original. Wheat tended to be more consistent, though its subtle changes can be traced from an earlier, lighter, slightly whitish yellow, to a more golden yellow after World War II and into the 1950s. By the late 1950s, Wheat had evolved into an icier yellow with an almost greenish cast. (2001, 10)

The following chronology illustrates the progression of finishes used on Heywood-Wakefield's Streamlined Modern and Modern furniture. Following the chronology is a list of each finish for which a company definition could be located.

1935 – Walma finish is used on many of the earliest pieces in the Modern line.

1936-37 – Amber, Bleached, and Modern Walnut offered as finishes. In addition, a combination of Amber and Bleached was available on some case pieces with draw-ers. When this combination option was selected, the out-side and frame of the case (plus the drawer pulls) were finished in Amber, while the drawer fronts were finished in Bleached. (The Penthouse group on page 171 illus-trates several pieces finished in this way.) Catalog copy notes that non case pieces (such as beds, mirrors, cof-fee tables, etc.) could only be ordered in either all Am-ber or all Bleached; the rounded, streamlined edges of these pieces would make it impossible to achieve effec-tive color separation needed for the combination finish.

1937 – Wheat finish first developed by Heywood-Wakefield. Company literature describes it as an "overnight sensa-tion … [that] brought to Modern the one remaining qual-ity it needed … the charm and character of a lively color."

1939 – Primary finishes are Wheat, Champagne, and Amber. Bleached and Modern Walnut still available upon request.

1940 – Champagne (described in the catalog as "now, our most popular finish"), Wheat, and No. 2. Walnut are of-fered. No. 2 Walnut was recommended primarily for chairs that would be used in combination with additional walnut pieces purchased from other manufacturers.

1941 – Heywood-Wakefield advertises "Your Choice of Two Lovely, *Livable*, Finishes," Wheat or Champagne. Champagne is described as a good choice for upholstered pieces that in-clude blues, turquoise, sage green or yellow in the fabric.

1944 – Wheat or Champagne are available on the Revised Basic Line of wartime furniture offerings.

1950-53 – Wheat and Champagne are regular finishes. Spe-cial finishes are Winthrop, Priscilla Maple, Mahogany or Walnut (latter two on full upholstered patterns only).

1954 – Wheat, Champagne, and Platinum are regular fin-ishes. Special finishes include Winthrop, Priscilla Maple, and Monticello; Mahogany or Walnut still available on full upholstered patterns.

1955 – Wheat, Champagne, Platinum, Sable Grey, Toast, and Nut Brown are available (the latter two available on Dakar line only).

1956 – Wheat, Champagne, Platinum, Sable Grey, and Toast are regular finishes. (Toast available on solid Mahogany only, i.e., the Dakar line). Winthrop and Cinnamon (typi-cally used on the Old Colony line) are also available, but not recommended due to differences in wood selection between Old Colony and Modern.

1957 – Wheat, Sherry, Champagne, and Sable Grey are regu-lar finishes.

1958 – Wheat, Champagne, Sable Grey, Platinum, Fruitwood, Tampico, and Black are regular finishes. (Black available only on the legs of full upholstered pieces.)

1958 – Finishes on the Cadence and Encore lines are the same as the 1958 list above (excluding Black), with the addition of Topaz.

1959 – The Cadence line offers Wheat, Champagne, Sable Grey, Platinum, Fruitwood, Topaz, or Walnut as finishes.

1960 – The Encore line offers Wheat, Champagne, Sable Grey, Platinum, Fruitwood, Topaz, or Walnut.

1962 – The Encore line offers Wheat, Champagne, Topaz, Walnut, Westwood, and Windsor as regular finishes. Cinnamon and Olde Salem (Old Colony finishes) are not recommended.

Finish definitions, as found in company literature
(listed chronologically in approximate order of introduction):

WALMA – a two-tone type of finish with a soft, warm, deep tan effect on the Quilted Maple parts of the furniture and a rich, deep brown on the Plain Striped Walnut sections.

AMBER – a warm mellow maple color.

BLEACHED – a clear, sparkling blond tone.

No. 2 WALNUT – a pleasing neutral tone walnut.

WHEAT – a yellow cast that resembles the color of ripened wheat grain.

CHAMPAGNE – a pink tone that resembles the color of a correctly-made champagne cocktail.

PLATINUM – a neutral blond color with overtones of light gray and light beige blended to a handsome hue.

SABLE GREY – a medium gray color, clear in tone and transparent in character to bring out the distinctive grain of the solid birch wood. It is not a muddy gray color so common to open grain woods.

TOAST – a light brown finish, transparent in tone and application, that brings out the distinctive grain of solid Mahogany wood.

SHERRY – a soft, mellow tone in the brown family of fine furniture finishes.

FRUITWOOD – a warm walnut-tone of distinctive clarity and brilliance.

TAMPICO – a soft beige color slightly darker than Platinum. It is a light nutmeg color of unusual depth and rich patina.

TOPAZ – a mellow golden-brown tone which enriches the beautiful birch wood grain.

WALNUT – a dark walnut-tone transparent finish that accentuates the exquisite grain of our solid birch wood.

WESTWOOD – a natural light honey-tone finish that is exceptionally transparent to show off the distinctive grain of the solid birch wood.

WINDSOR – a warm brown tone, evenly applied and transparent in color that brings out the clean, clear tone of the solid birch wood grain.

Identification

Heywood-Wakefield marked its Streamline Modern and Modern furniture using paper labels and/or ink stamps. The labels (either a woodgrain style or a red, white, and blue style) were used prior to 1946 and were glued onto the back or underside of the furniture. In 1946, the company adopted the eagle in a circle trademark and began branding or stamping their furniture with this trademark (which can be found on the back, underside, or in a top drawer).

Both before and after the war, the style code and finish color were also stamped on each piece, generally on the back or underside. Prewar style codes begin with a letter C, followed by at least four digits and sometimes one or more additional letters to indicate the type of furniture (e.g., C 3341, C 2698-66, or C 2707 G). Postwar style codes begin with an M, followed by at least three digits and/or one or more additional letters (e.g., M 755, M 1167-52, or M 6107 A). As noted earlier, Aristocraft style numbers begin with a CM (e.g., CM 368).

A page from Heywood-Wakefield's 1941 brochure for Streamline Modern, promoting the company's two most successful finishes.

Index

This index is divided into two sections—one for the 1930s and 1940s (model numbers beginning with "C") and one for the 1950s (model numbers beginning with "M" and "CM"). Within each section, the items are organized numerically by model number. Items marked "NS" are not shown in this book but are included here for reference.

1930s and 1940s

CM 728-44	Love Seat (Aristocraft), 90	
CM 729-66	Davenport (Aristocraft), 91	
M 730	Bed (Tempo), 215	
M 731	Single Dresser (Tempo), 225	
M 731-525	Dresser with Attached Mirror (Tempo), 225	
M 732	4-Drawer Chest (Tempo), 226	
M 734	Double Dresser (Tempo), 226	
M 734-525	Double Dresser with Attached Mirror (Tempo) (NS)	
M 734-575	Double Dresser with Attached Mirror (Tempo) (NS)	
M 736	Desk/Vanity (Tempo), 235	
M 738	Night Stand (Tempo), 218	
M 739	Triple Dresser (Tempo), 226	
M 739-525	Triple Dresser with Attached Mirror (Tempo) (NS)	
M 739-575	Triple Dresser with Attached Mirror (Tempo) (NS)	
M 740	Utility Headboard Bed (Tempo), 215	
M 740 (6' 6")	Double Utility Headboard (Tempo), 215	
M 740 X	Utility Headboard with Footboard (Tempo) (NS)	
M 742	5-Drawer Chest (Tempo), 226	
M 755	Single Filler, 69	
M 755 C	Arm Chair, 70	
M 755 LC/RC	Left or Right Arm Chair, 69	
M 756	Double Filler, 70	
M 756 LC/RC	Double Filler with Right or Left Arm, 70	
M 756-48	Love Seat, 70	
M 758-68	Davenport, 70	
M 770	Bed (Sculptura), 213	
M 770 H	Footless Bed (Sculptura), 213	
M 770 (6' 6")	Headboard Bed (Sculptura), 213	
M 771	Single Dresser (Sculptura), 222	
M 771-525	Dresser with Attached Mirror (Sculptura) (NS)	
M 771-573	Dresser with Attached Mirror (Sculptura), 222	
M 772	Chest (Sculptura), 222	
M 774	Mr. & Mrs. Dresser (Sculptura), 223	
M 774-525	Mr. & Mrs. Dresser with Attached Mirror (Sculptura) (NS)	
M 774-575	Mr. & Mrs. Dresser with Attached Mirror (Sculptura), 223	
M 776	Deluxe Vanity (Sculptura), 234	
M 777	Vanity Bench (Sculptura), 234	
M 778	Night Stand (Sculptura), 218	
M 779	Triple Dresser (Sculptura), 223	
M 779-525	Triple Dresser with Attached Mirror (Sculptura) (NS)	
M 779-575	Triple Dresser with Attached Mirror (Sculptura), 223	
M 780	Cabinet Utility Headboard (Encore), 212	
M 781	Deck Top (Sculptura), 222	
M 782 W	Utility Case, 163	
M 783 W	Student's Desk, 111	
M 785	Large Open Hutch, 162	
M 786 G	Pedestal Extension Table, 142	
M 787 G	Game Dining Table, 143	
M 788 G	Extension Game Dining Table, 143	
M 789 G	Large Dining Extension Table, 143	
M 790	Utility Headboard (Encore), 212	
M 790 (6' 6")	Double Utility Headboard (Encore), 212	
M 791 G	End Table, 102	
M 792	5-Drawer Chest (Sculptura), 223	
M 793 G	Lamp Table with Drawer, 95	
M 794 G	Step-End Table with Drawer, 104	
M 795 G	Large Cocktail Table, 98	
M 797 C	High Back Barrel Chair, 50	
M 798 C	Open Arm Posture Back Arm Chair, 50	
M 799 C	Posture Back Arm Chair, 50	
M 902 G	Nest of Tables, 109	
M 905 G	Cocktail Table with Drawers, 98	
M 906 G	Wedge Step-End Table, 104	
M 908 G	Step-End Table, 105	
M 909	China Top, 164	
M 910	Bed (Harmonic), 214	
M 911	3-Drawer Dresser (Harmonic), 223	
M 911-525	Dresser with Attached Mirror (Harmonic) (NS)	
M 911-573	Dresser with Attached Mirror (Harmonic) (NS)	
M 912	5-Drawer Chest (Harmonic), 223	
M 914	Mr. and Mrs. Dresser (Harmonic), 223	
M 916	Desk/Vanity (Harmonic), 234	
M 918	Night Stand (Harmonic), 218	
M 920	Bed (Encore), 212	
M 923	Chest Mirror, 235	
M 926	Vanity/Desk (Encore), 233	
CM 927	Single Filler (Aristocraft), 91	
CM 927 C	Arm Chair (Aristocraft), 91	
CM 927 LC/RC	Left or Right Arm Chair (Aristocraft), 91	
CM 928	Double Filler (Aristocraft), 92	
CM 928 LC/RC	Double Filler with Left or Right Arm (Aristocraft), 93	
CM 928-44	Love Seat (Aristocraft), 93	
CM 929-66	Davenport (Aristocraft), 93	
M 930	Bed (Encore), 212	
CM 931	Double Filler (Aristocraft), 92	
CM 931 LC/RC	Double Filler with Right or Left Arm (Aristocraft), 92	
CM 931-44	Love Seat (Aristocraft), 92	
CM 931-50	Love Seat (Aristocraft), 93	
CM 932-66	Davenport (Aristocraft), 92	
CM 932-72	Davenport (Aristocraft), 93	
M 934	Starter Chest, 111	
M 934 W	Starter Chest with Desk Drawer, 111	
M 935	Single Filler, 71	
M 935 C	Arm Chair, 72	
M 935 LC/RC	Left or Right Arm Chair, 71	
M 936	Double Filler, 72	
M 936 LC/RC	Double Filler with Right or Left Arm, 72	
M 936-48	Love Seat, 72	
M 937-84	Davenport Sleeper, 72	
M 938 G	Corner Table, 107	
M 941 C	Arm Chair, 50	
M 945 C	Club/Lounge Chair, 51	
M 946 C	Ladies' Chair, 51	
M 947 C	Lounge Chair, 51	
M 948	Armless Pull-Up Chair, 51	
M 950 G	Round Extension Table, 143	
M 952 G	Plastic Top Dining Extension Table, 144	
M 953 A	Side Chair, 153	
M 953 C	Arm Chair, 153	
M 955	Single Filler, 65	
M 955 C	Arm Chair, 65	
M 955 LC/RC	Left or Right Arm Chair, 65	
M 956	Double Filler, 65	
M 956 LC/RC	Double Filler with Left or Right Arm, 65	
M 956-48	Love Seat, 66	
M 958-68	Davenport, 66	
M 960	Single Filler, 66	
M 960 C	Arm Chair (NS)	
M 960 LC/RC	Left or Right Arm Chair, 66	

M 1578 G	Round Cocktail Table, 99	M 1785	Single Filler (Monterey), 82
M 1579 G	Square Cocktail Table, 99	M 1785 C	Arm Chair (Monterey), 83
M 1580 G	Cocktail Table, 100	M 1785 RC/LC	Right or Left Arm Chair (Monterey), 83
M 1581 G	Cocktail Table with Shelf, 100	M 1786	Double Filler (Monterey), 83
M 1582	5-Drawer Chest (Encore), 230	M 1786 RC/LC	Right or Left Arm Sofa (Monterey), 83
M 1583 G	Lamp Table, 96	M 1786-56	Love Seat (Monterey), 83
M 1584 G	Step-End Table, 106	M 1787-80	Sofa (Monterey), 83
M 1585 G	Large Cocktail Table with Drawer, 100	M 1788	Quarter Round (Monterey/Gramercy Park), 85
M 1586 G	Lamp Table, 96	M 1789 R or L	Right or Left Bumper End-off (Monterey/Gramercy Park), 85
M 1587 G	Drop-Leaf Utility Table, 109	M 1790	Single Filler (Gramercy Park), 84
M 1588 G	Lamp Table, 96	M 1790 C	Arm Chair (Gramercy Park), 85
M 1589 G	Large Dining Extension Table, 147	M 1790 RC/LC	Right or Left Arm Chair (Gramercy Park), 84
M 1590 G	Corner Table, 107	M 1791	Double Filler (Gramercy Park), 84
M 1592	Tambour Buffet, 167	M 1791 RC/LC	Right or Left Arm Sofa (Gramercy Park), 84
M 1593 A	Side Chair, 159	M 1791-60	Love Seat (Gramercy Park), 85
M 1594 A	Side Chair, 159	M 1792-84	Sofa (Gramercy Park), 85
M 1594 C	Arm Chair, 159	M 1793-96	Pillow-Back Sofa (Gramercy Park), 85
M 1596	Glass Door Hutch Top, 167	M 1794 C	Ladies' Chair, 53
M 1596/M 1542	Glass Door Hutch Top on Tambour Buffet, 167	M 1796 C	Pillow-Back Arm Chair, 53
M 1597	Server/Storage Chest, 167	M 1920 H	Paneled Headboard Bed (Encore), 217
M 1598	Glass Door Hutch, 167	M 1921	Straight Bookcase, 113
M 1598/M 1597	Glass Door Hutch on Server, 167	M 1922	Corner Bookcase, 113
CM 1701 G	Cocktail Table (Aristocraft), 101	M 1923	Corner Desk, 111
CM 1702 G	End Table (Aristocraft), 103	M 1924	Wall Cabinet, 114
CM 1703 G	Lamp Table (Aristocraft), 96	M 1925	Corner Cabinet, 114
CM 1704 G	Step-End Table (Aristocraft), 106	M 1930	Bookcase Headboard Bed (Encore), 216
CM 1707 G	Corner Table (Aristocraft), 108	M 1932	4-Drawer Chest (Symphonic), 231
M 1710	Panel Bed (Dakar), 215	M 1934	Double Dresser (Symphonic), 231
M 1710 H	Footless Bed (Dakar) (NS)	M 1934-1533	Double Dresser with Attached Mirror (Symphonic), 231
M 1711	Vanity Chest (Dakar), 235	M 1934-1535	Double Dresser with Attached Mirror (Symphonic) (NS)
M 1711 W	Vanity Chest with Desk Drawer (Dakar) (NS)		
M 1712	4-Drawer Chest (Dakar), 227	M 1938	Night Table (Symphonic), 219
M 1713	Hanging Mirror (Dakar), 235	M 1939	Triple Dresser (Symphonic), 231
M 1714	Double Dresser (Dakar), 227	M 1939-1533	Triple Dresser with Attached Mirror (Symphonic) (NS)
M 1714 W	Double Dresser with Vanity/Desk Drawer (Dakar), 227	M 1939-1535	Triple Dresser with Attached Mirror (Symphonic), 231
M 1714-1715	Double Dresser with Attached Mirror (Dakar), 227	M 1940	Utility Headboard Bed (Encore), 217
M 1716	Vanity (Dakar), 235	M 3753 G	Step-End Table (West Coast pattern), 104
M 1717	Vanity Bench (Dakar), 235	M 5608 C	Club Chair (West Coast pattern), 64
M 1718	Night Stand (Dakar), 218	M 5608 L & R	Left and Right Arm Sectional (West Coast pattern), 64
M 1719	Triple Dresser (Dakar), 227	M 5608 LR	Leg Rest (West Coast pattern), 63
M 1719 W	Triple Dresser with Vanity/Desk Drawer (Dakar) (NS)	M 5608-28	Single Filler (West Coast pattern), 63
M 1719-1715	Triple Dresser with Attached Mirror (Dakar), 227	M 5608-95	Armless Davenport (West Coast pattern), 64
M 1720	Utility Headboard Bed (Dakar), 215	M 5608-100	Davenport (West Coast pattern), 64
M 1720 X	Utility Headboard Bed with Footboard (Dakar) (NS)	M 5628-78	Davenport (West Coast pattern), 64
M 1722	5-Drawer Chest (Dakar), 228	M 6107 A	Side Chair (West Coast pattern), 152
M 1730	Utility Headboard Bed with End Compartments (Dakar), 215	M 6107 C	Arm Chair (West Coast pattern), 152
M 1730 X	Utility Headboard Bed with End Compartments & Footboard (Dakar) (NS)	M 6321 G	Cocktail Table (West Coast pattern), 98